WHAT PEOPLE ARE SAYING
ABOUT *MATURE-ISH* . . .

For too long, the focus of calling has been primarily on pastors, but the reality is that everyone in the Body of Christ has been called. This book will serve as an incredible guide by an incredible leader to help you find and fulfill your call. I love that it intertwines our calling and our walks with the Lord. Read this and learn; practice it and grow.

Bob Roberts, Global Senior Pastor, Northwood Church
Author, *Bold as Love: What Can Happen When We See People the Way God Does*

I LOVE this book! No matter what stage of your spiritual journey, you will be encouraged and challenged to deeper spiritual growth. In this book, Bill White gives you practical understanding on what it takes to go to the next level with a greater sense of purpose.

Jim Burns, PhD, President, HomeWord
Author of *Doing Life With Your Adult Children: Keep Your Mouth Shut and the Welcome Mat Out*

Every once in a while, you start reading a book and you cannot put it down. This is one such book. WOW! What a God-inspired writing. It is life-changing with a blueprint on the various stages of Christian growth. Dr. Bill, you are really a blessed man of God who He is using to make an impact.

Albert E. Dotson, Sr., PhD, Chairman Emeritus, 100 Black Men in America; Former President, Orange Bowl Committee; Deacon, Sweet Home Missionary Baptist Church, Miami, Florida

Pastor Bill White is a voice I trust. He paints a beautiful picture of how your faith can grow in any season or stage of life. *Mature-ish* is a refreshing read for all, no matter where you are in your walk with Christ. New believers will be stretched to take bold steps in their faith, and seasoned believers will be challenged to finish the race strong.

Ted Cunningham, Pastor, Woodland Hills Family Church, Branson, Missouri
Author, *Fun Loving You*

Bill White has done it again! Writing from the vantage point of a seasoned pastor who genuinely believes the Gospel is Good News to people at every stage of life, Bill has created a compelling metaphor for our faith journey. In his typically direct and engaging style, Bill makes the case that growing in Christ is a life-long adventure to embrace and transform the various challenges we all face. This journey with Christ is at the heart of what it means to claim the name of Christian. This book will be a wonderful asset for all those who believe the journey is the secret to both abundant and eternal life.

Bill Wilson, Director, The Center for Healthy Churches

Pastor Bill White captivated me when he summarized the reason he wrote this book: to help me achieve my most significant desire—*fulfilling God's mission for my life.* In typical pastoral fashion, Bill biblically, illustratively, and precisely walks you through the goals, challenges, and course corrections of every stage in the God-directed life journey. For those who want to fulfill God's mission for their lives, *if you choose to accept it, Mature-ish* provides the pathway forward.

Jim Tomberlin, Pastor, Author, Church Strategist

In the 45 years I've known Bill, his greatest desire has always been to know God's will and do it . . . whether anyone else did or not! He used to tease me (in a good way) about being a "mama's boy." But as you will discover in this book, the ferocity and tenderness of God's "mama love" makes all the difference.

David Ring, Author and Evangelist

Mature-ish is the right book, with the right thoughts, messages and challenges, at the right time in our world today. How brilliant to align the stages of our spiritual growth with those of our physical and psychological growth! It speaks to our *intellect* by educating, to our *soul* with the opportunity for reflection, and to tangible progress in our spiritual journey with course corrections that will guide us. This "connect the dots" approach to spiritual growth will make a difference in your life. And for me, knowing that we are not perfect yet always striving to grow in our faith, the ability to always reach out to *Mature-ish* for guidance will be comforting and uplifting. So, in Pastor Bill's words, "stay curious, stay real, and stay at it" as you embark upon or continue on your spiritual growth journey.

Ana Lopez-Blazquez, Executive VP, Chief Strategy & Transformation Officer, Baptist Health South Florida, CEO Baptist Health Enterprises

When I first met Bill, he was 18 and illegally climbing through a window into my church! Though it was an unusual introduction, I had the joy of watching his personal relationship with Christ blossom and grow since that day. So, while reading this book and reminiscing on Bill's journey with Christ, I was constantly reminded of a recurring theme in the Scriptures that's still true today. You see, Noah looked crazy to everyone who saw him; Joseph appeared abandoned by his brothers; Mary was young, pregnant and unwed, and Bill was attempting unlawful entry. What seemed wrong or out of place to man was a step toward the amazing will of God that, to this day, continues to transform so many lives. It is my prayer that this book will help guide you to the maturity Christ has in store for you, trusting and resting in the knowledge that God is stronger, wiser and more loving than any of your life's circumstances.

Pastor Ken Dodson, MEd, MA, LPC

In my quest to become the mission-minded minister God has prepared me to be, I have always been in awe of how God has worked in my life. Bill's book is a sacred tool that shows in a practical, profound, and personal way how the hand of God guides us so that we fulfill our mission in life. One point in particular makes this book a must read . . . "progress happens according to a process." I highly recommend this book to show you how to fulfill your life's mission.

Rev. Dr. Carl Johnson, Pastor, 93rd Street Community Baptist Church, Miami, Chaplain, Florida Highway Patrol Department, State Moderator, Florida General Baptist Convention

I whole-heartedly recommend this book for a clearer understanding of the stages of maturing in Christ. It doesn't matter where you are in life, as one of our dear clients in the Agape Community or those who are incarcerated, it guides you through your God-given journey to become more like Christ.

Rev. Dr. Jose Hernandez, Founder, South Florida Jail Ministries & Agape Network, Retired Commander Chaplaincy Services Bureau, Miami-Dade Corrections and Rehabilitation Department

I worked with Pastor Bill White as his Executive Assistant for seven years. During that time, I experienced his deep conviction and love for Jesus. Although he went through many trials, temptations and tribulations, I always saw him standing in faith and the strength of the Lord. One thing I admire about him as a leader and man of authority is that he encourages others to step into the purpose and destiny God has for them. He was instrumental in helping me do that. And in this book, he will do the same for you!

Betty Lara, Executive Director, Glory House of Miami, Inc.

Dr. Bill White has provided a thoughtful and practical guide to discipleship and spiritual maturity. This biblically sound book examines the path to growth and fruitfulness in our Christian walk in a clear and concise manner.

Pastor Erik D. Cummings, Lead Pastor, New Life Church of Carol City, and President, Florida Baptist Convention

What is your mind-blowing mission from God? Bill White's *Mature-ish* gives us an adventure manual to explore the most significant accomplishment of our lives . . . our mission from on high. In stages from newborn to godparent, we learn what it means to come alive in the Spirit. In my own life, Bill White has encouraged me to do just that—come alive in the Spirit. He has always embraced a God-sized vision as a city leader and pastor. I am so thankful to have him in my life. I highly recommend this, his latest book.

Chris Lane, Executive Director for Miami, National Christian Foundation South Florida

MATURE-ish

Your mission from God, should you choose to accept it...

BILL WHITE

ISBNs:
Print: 978-1-947505-32-2
Digital: 978-1-947505-33-9

Cover design by Cindy Cohen, Maggen Creative, Inc.
Interior design by Anne McLaughlin, Blue Lake Design
Published by Baxter Press, Friendswood, Texas

Printed in the United States

To my parents, William L. and LaVeta M. White, who,

following God's call to "Go West!" shared the gospel , their love,

and their lives with the Native American people in Arizona:

Navajo, Hopi, Papago, Pima, Apache, Cherokee and Cheyenne.

CONTENTS

PREFACE

Who knew when 2020 rolled around that we would be spending the majority of it under "shelter at home" directions because of the Covid-19 pandemic? What a very different year than any of us anticipated! Though our church has chosen to be physically distanced, we have stayed spiritually connected through live streaming and digital ministry. Thank God that back in 2011 He granted us vision to launch our online ministries.

I am also thankful that this year provided me with the opportunity to develop this framework for fullness that Scripture gives for our spiritual growth. This volume is meant to be companion to my first book, *Upside Down Kingdom*, providing actionable next steps for each Christ-follower to take in order to grow in being "filled to the measure of all the fullness of God." May your capacity for God expand in every way as you undertake this journey.

Bill White

INTRODUCTION

Did you know that during the Apollo 11 mission to the moon fifty years ago, the spacecraft was actually off-course ninety percent of the time! Charles Garfield, computer scientist with NASA during the first moon landing, notes this remarkable fact in his book, *Peak Performers*.[1] If the astronauts were off-course so much of the time, how were they able to fulfill their mission? Course corrections. Rapid course corrections! Through constant communication with Mission Control, they were able to make all the necessary adjustments in real time, and they ultimately succeeded in spite of the challenges. By the way, the smartphone in your pocket uses technology that's 100,000 times more powerful than what was available in 1969.[2] The moon landing has been heralded as perhaps the most significant accomplishment of the twentieth century, but it could only happen because smart people made countless corrections along the way.

This book has been written to help you fulfill the most significant accomplishment of your life: your mission from God, should you choose to accept it.

If you have ever longed for a tool to help you mark your progress in fulfilling your life mission from God, this book is humbly placed in your hands to that end. It provides a framework to equip you to pilot and monitor your own spiritual advance. It's also an adventure manual to help set and maintain your course during your mission.

In the United States space program, Mission Control had a very clear purpose and plan for each launch. The Apollo 11 astronauts fulfilled their purpose to land on the moon and come back because they stayed in contact with Mission Control and followed their plan. God is Mission Control for us. We can be sure that His purpose is better than anything we can imagine, even if His plan sometimes takes us in directions we can't immediately comprehend. That's the nature of a real adventure!

Our mission has two spheres of influence: internal and external. God has a plan for us to grow, learn, and develop our "inner space," and we have the privilege of representing Him to the people around us. (No, they're not in "outer space," but you get the idea.)

How magnificent is God's mission? The apostle Paul described it in one of his letters to Christians. He said that God wants us to "grasp how wide and long and high and deep is the love of Christ and to know this love that surpasses knowledge—that you may be filled to the measure of all the fullness of God" (Ephesians 3:18-19).

This is mind-blowing! What does it mean to be "filled to the measure of all the fullness of God"? I'm sure I don't fully know, but if the God of the heavens wants me "to be filled to the measure of all the fullness of God," I'm all in!

Stages

In this book, I'll identify and describe ten stages of spiritual growth. How fast will you progress through the stages of growth? It all depends on how you use what God gives you, and how much, how soon, how deeply and truly you listen to Mission Control and make your mid-course corrections. You're the pilot, and you set your own pace.

Spiritual maturity isn't a matter of how long you have walked with God, but of how truly you are applying His Word. It's possible to have the best plan and the most detailed map and still be going nowhere. But when you act, you reach your destination and fulfill your mission. My prayer is that God will use this book as a tool, mapping a path forward for you and those He calls you to help on their journey.

You'll notice that the book is presented in a linear growth format from the beginning to full maturity. As you look at the stages and the chapter titles, you may realize you're farther along than just beginning. Feel free to fast forward and skip to the chapter that fits your journey now. To those of us actively mentoring others, I hope you will find the chapters suited for stimulating conversation and guiding growth in the eager disciples you serve.

Erik Erikson was a twentieth-century psychologist who created a theory that each stage of life (he identified eight stages) can be associated with a discrete psychological struggle related to the development of personality. Working through each of the struggles results in a new basic virtue. Erikson's stages were associated with age ranges, although progress had less to do with age than with the ability to deal with each successive struggle.

Erikson connected the social and psychological aspects of maturity, and I believe we can take a similar approach to *spiritual* maturity, as shown on the following chart. In my ministry through the years, I've noticed that people progress through a process in their journey toward mature faith. We start on the bottom as a spiritual newborn and then, hopefully, continue to mature throughout our lives.

Progress happens according to a process, but keep in mind that these stages of spiritual growth may not correlate with physical development. For instance, a great-grandfather in the biological sense may be a "newborn" Christian, while young people may show surprising levels of spiritual maturity. The simple chart below indicates how God has designed that we move up and to the right as we "become mature, attaining to the whole measure of the fullness of Christ."

Maturity on Mission from God

Stage 10	Godparent
Stage 9	Grandparent
Stage 8	Parent
Stage 7	Adult
Stage 6	Adolescent
Stage 5	Preteen
Stage 4	Child
Stage 3	Toddler
Stage 2	Infant
Stage 1	Newborn

I think of it this way:

➤ People in the first three stages—Newborn, Infant, and Toddler—are saying "feed me."

➤ People in the three next stages—Child, Preteen, and Adolescent—are saying "equip me."

➤ And people in the last four stages—Adult, Parent, Grandparent, and Godparent—are saying "follow me."

At Stage 8 of this process I will also offer my observations regarding stages of unbelief. There you'll find a list of resources to help pre-believers navigate through the stages of unbelief toward their own saving relationship with Christ.

Course Changes

Each chapter is followed by "adventure pages" in three parts: The Pilot's Flight Plan includes questions for you to consider regarding your personal growth; Course Correction has one action point that fits that stage and helps you take steps toward the next level; and a Captain's Log offers advice for mentors and coaches who are helping people take the next step in their growth.

I'm calling this book Mature-*ish*. Most growing Christians squirm a bit if asked, "Are you spiritually mature?" We always have a little (or a lot) further to go, don't we? We always could do a little better, and it may sound arrogant or presumptuous to say, "Why, yes indeed, I am spiritually mature!" The truth is that we're always working on it, doing our best, making progress. Even when we've made significant progress, we're not to the finish line yet, but we're mature . . . ish.

So, where are you on the journey? How mature-ish are you spiritually? Are you ready to identify the necessary course corrections that will propel you to your next level? Are you tired of being stuck? Of feeling stalled or aimless in your spiritual journey? Are you open and willing to receive God's life-giving truth?

I'm assuming the answers to these questions is "Yes!" Then know this: my prayers and those of Christ Journey Church and our intercessory prayer warriors are with you as you accept your mission from God and grow to "become mature, attaining to the whole measure of the fullness of Christ."

THERE'S NOTHING LIKE NEW LIFE!

NEWBORN

"Babies are such a nice way to start people."

—Dan Herold

It's an astounding thing—a deep and wonderful truth—that God longs to love each one of us as our "Abba." Jesus said He came to help us know and experience God as Father, to pour His powerful and personal relationship with God, whom He knows as His Heavenly Father, into our lives.

Abba is one of the most tender and intimate words for father in the Bible. In Aramaic, it means "Daddy!" When Jesus cries out to God in the Garden of Gethsemane before going to the cross, He prays, "*Abba*, Father, everything is possible for you" (Mark 14:36).

Amazingly, Almighty God wants to love you and me as a daddy loves His children. Imagine this with me and ask God to help you feel what it means. God is so full of love for you and so full of dreams for you that He would come to earth as one of us—to redeem, restore, and release you into the full adventure of new life in Him. This is my prayer: "Lord, open our eyes to the plan You have for each of us!"

Reaching, Stretching, Growing

What is it about children that they always seem to be on their way to the next level? Have you noticed? Whatever age they are, they're still on their way. "I'm four. My next birthday I'll be five." Or, "I'm six *and a half*!" Or, "I'm *almost* eight." There's something about a healthy child that compels them to keep an eye on where they're going, not simply where they've been or where they are.

It's the same with healthy spiritual children. They somehow know that where they are and where they've been is not where they're supposed to stay. They're on their way, growing through to the next level. God wants all His children to be on their way, to grow up in productive, healthy, and joyful maturity toward fulfilling their mission in life. But it all starts somewhere. It starts with knowing God as the giver of life and experiencing your new life in Christ. Your spiritual journey begins with your receiving new life in Christ from *Abba*, your spiritual daddy.

You probably wouldn't be reading this book if you weren't already interested in how you can grow spiritually, but Jesus taught that spiritual growth is about much more than religion with its rituals and rules, and much more than an ethereal "spirituality" or an esoteric philosophy promising to connect you to the universe. Jesus taught us we need more than New Age. We need new life. We need new birth.

Where It All Begins

As in physical life, spiritual life also begins with birth. When the curious Pharisee Nicodemus sought out Jesus to discuss spiritual matters, Jesus told him, "Very truly I tell you, no one can see the kingdom of God unless they are born again" (John 3:3). Nicodemus was bewildered. His religious training hadn't prepared him to understand, and his confusion was compounded when he tried to take Jesus too literally. But Jesus explained that He was speaking about a *spiritual* birth (John 3:5-6).

To Jesus, it's one thing to be born physically, but it's entirely another to come alive in the Spirit.

To Jesus, it's one thing to be born physically, but it's entirely another to come alive in the Spirit. So, the question is: have you been born in the Spirit? That's the action that initiates your spiritual life and growth. Jesus wants everybody to come alive with *Abba*'s spiritual life, and it all begins with new birth. (For more about how to be born again, please refer to the appendix).

Jesus affirmed that human beings have the amazing capacity not only to grow physically, but at the same time, to come alive and grow spiritually. This chapter is about how to grow as a spiritual newborn.

One of the wonderful privileges I have as a pastor is getting to celebrate new babies being welcomed into the families of countless couples through the years. The wonder and miracle of a newborn baby never gets old! Few things in life compare with what parents feel when looking into their new baby's eyes! Then, soon enough, every parent also understands why the newborn stage has been called "a time when nobody sleeps, everybody smells, and a very small person who can't really speak still has the power to convince you, 'I need you now!'"

The famous African proverb reminds us, "It takes a village to raise a child." Our church loves being that village, helping families and partnering with parents for their child's growth. When anyone in our church has a new baby, we immediately welcome the little one into our church family. On a typical Sunday morning at each of our campuses, a team of highly trained and background-checked leaders, led by our outstanding Family Ministry team, provide care for our smallest and most vulnerable Christ Journey family members. Our Coral Gables campus preschool director, Jenny Estrada, calls these littlest ones "baby geniuses" because their minds are so open to the world. From the earliest ages and stages of these little ones' lives, our dedicated caregivers cover them in prayer, sing worship songs to them, and whisper Scripture into their tiny ears.

It's so frustrating that in the current pandemic (I sure hope it's over by the time you read this!), we aren't able to get together to ooh and aah over our new babies. A baby's birth is a time to celebrate together and shower the child and the parents with love. We can hardly wait to do that again in person.

Meanwhile, we continue to acknowledge the dual celebration of new physical life and the anticipation of the spiritual journey for newborns in our community. One of our members who is a nurse oversees our blanket ministry at a local hospital where we provide a gift blanket to every newborn. We want each family to feel the warmth of God's love and the covering blessing of prayer. We care for the physical needs of the child and parents, but we don't neglect the importance of their spiritual needs.

What are the needs of a newborn? At the risk of extreme oversimplification, I'd like to suggest three that apply to both physical and spiritual newborns, but I'll focus on the impact they have in spiritual growth. A newborn needs loving, feeding, and changing!

A spiritual newborn needs to be loved.

The First Need of a Newborn

First, a spiritual newborn needs to be loved. Just as physical babies need to feel loved, valued, and affirmed by their parents, siblings, and grandparents, spiritual newborns need to know and feel the love of God for them in their spiritual family, the Church. It's little wonder that almost every author of the New Testament calls on God's people to encourage one another in God's love!

In his letter to the Romans, the Apostle Paul lays it out like this for God's children of every age: "I am convinced that nothing can ever separate us from God's love. Neither death nor life, neither angels nor demons, neither our fears for today nor our worries about tomorrow—not even the powers of hell can separate us from God's love. No power in the sky above or in the earth below—indeed, nothing in all creation will ever be able to separate us from the love of God that is revealed in Christ Jesus our Lord" (Romans 8:38-39 NLT). Spiritual newborns especially need to know they are unconditionally treasured and deeply connected in *Abba's* unshakeable love.

The Apostle Peter similarly cheers on the young church scattered across the Roman Empire with these words, "So now you must show sincere love to each other as brothers and sisters. Love each other deeply with all your heart" (1 Peter 1:22 NLT). A little later in the same letter, he underlines the call again, "Most important of all, continue to show deep love for each other, for love covers a multitude of sins" (1 Peter 4:8 NLT). Every spiritual newborn needs the "love covers" to be pulled up around them in their new family of faith.

Every spiritual newborn needs the "love covers" to be pulled up around them in their new family of faith.

Paul has been called the apostle of faith, Peter, the apostle of hope, and John, the apostle of love. Here's what John wrote to the children of God in his care, "Dear friends, let us continue to love one another, for love comes from God . . . God is love, and all who live in love live in God . . . And he has given us this command: Those who love God must also love their fellow believers" (1 John 4:7, 16, 21 NLT).

So, to the spiritual caregivers and church leaders reading this right now, we must cultivate the community of love! How? By accepting, affirming, respecting, and valuing one another in Christ, and offering each other the love of our *Abba* Father in the same way we have received it from Him. God's spiritual babies must have plenty of love in order to grow! Please set the pace in helping new sisters and brothers know they are known, treasured, and needed in our family. Notice them. Introduce yourself. Invite them and include them in your group and activities, your Zoom calls and group chats. We all need to be loved, but those new in the faith especially do!

And for those who are spiritual newborns, please let yourself be loved. Don't isolate. Connect. Let yourself be known. Show up. Introduce yourself. Even if you feel shy or a little awkward (and who doesn't sometimes?), connecting to a group in the family for nurture and fellowship is God's birthright for you. Let yourself be loved and be assured that you belong, but don't stop there.

Ya Gotta Eat!

Newborns need loving, but they also need feeding. During the first few months of life, babies need to be held and fed almost constantly (at least, that's the way it seems). Child development expert, D. W. Winnicott once said, "There is no such thing as a baby, since a baby alone doesn't exist."[3] He means that it's impossible for a baby to exist without the care of nurturing parents or other caregivers.

A spiritual newborn needs to be fed.

A spiritual newborn needs to be fed. If you're new to the faith, feeding on God's Word is a must! For newborn and mature believers alike, staying well fed and nourished on Scripture is absolutely essential for spiritual health and wellness. Too many believers suffer from spiritual malnutrition because they've neglected a strong and balanced daily diet of truth from the Bible.

Jesus said, "People do not live by bread alone, but by every word that comes from the mouth of God" (Matthew 4:4 NLT). At the time, He was hungry following forty days of fasting, and He was responding to the devil's temptation to turn stones into bread. Jesus fought the tempter by affirming that His true nourishment came from God's Word. Seasoned spiritual warriors know that nourishing their spirits in God's Word daily is absolutely essential to spiritual health and strength.

God's faithful servant Job endured the heartache, confusion, and struggle of his multiple adversities. How? He explained, "I have not departed from his commands, but have treasured his words more than daily food" (Job 23:12 NLT). Jeremiah, known as the weeping prophet for the difficulties he faced as he grieved for his nation, found his heart encouraged. Where? "When I discovered your words, I devoured them. They are my joy and my heart's delight, for I bear your name, O Lord God of Heaven's Armies" (Jeremiah 15:16 NLT).

Where did King David find insight, sustenance, and stamina to perform the duties of leading his nation? In Psalm 19 he writes that God's Word in all its splendors was his resource for living and leading. He comments not only on the nutritional value but also on the flavor: "[The laws of the Lord] are sweeter than honey, even honey dripping from the comb!" (v. 10 NLT) In His Word, God has prepared a table before us, and we're to find replenishing nourishment there daily.

One of Jesus' final instructions to Peter was "Feed my lambs . . . Feed my sheep" (John 21:15, 17). Peter didn't forget that. In his first letter to encourage believers, he wrote, "Like newborn babies, you must crave pure spiritual milk so that you will grow into a full experience of salvation. Cry out for this nourishment, now that you have had a taste of the Lord's kindness" (1 Peter 2:2-3 NLT).

If the Bible had a nutritional facts panel like we find on the side of a cereal box about its contents, it could easily be 2 Timothy 3:16-17. In those verses Paul explains what God offers us in His Word: "All Scripture is God-breathed and is useful for teaching, rebuking, correcting and training in righteousness, so that the servant of God may be thoroughly equipped for every good work."

We can trust God's Word to be filled with God's life-giving nourishment. And when we take it into our minds and spirits, He will help us know how to live (teaching), when we get off track (rebuking) like a warning alarm on your car dashboard, how to get back on track (correcting), and how to stay on track and help others find their way (training and equipping). God's Word is an outfitter's shop and a field manual for your spiritual growth journey. And like Mission Control for Apollo 11, the Holy Spirit will guide you in making the necessary course corrections to help you fulfill your mission and accomplish God's plan for your life. (By the way, did you know that when Apollo 14 landed on the moon in 1971, the crew carried a Bible to the lunar surface? This fulfilled a desire of Apollo 1's Senior Pilot, Ed White.)

Jesus declared, "Heaven and earth will pass away, but my words will never pass away" (Matthew 24:35). Dear believer, whether you're seasoned in your walk with God or a fresh-from-the-womb spiritual newborn, God wants you to "Taste and see. The Lord is good!" (Psalm 34:8)

But how do we get this nourishment from the Bible? I recommend that you have two Bibles, one to read in a translation you find easy to understand, and another to study. At our church we recommend the *New International Version Life Application Study Bible* because its notes help provide trustworthy answers about what the Bible means and how it applies to your life. But you should also have a Bible that's easy to read. I recommend getting the free YouVersion Bible app. It has multiple translations in many languages, with audio available. The ones I listen to most are NIVUK, NLT, and MSG. We offer it on our free Christ Journey app, so you can easily access it there along with helpful tools from our church.

"First light. First choice. Seek first God's kingdom."

Let me tell you my personal practice. I have a place in my home where I start each day with Bible reading and prayer. "First light. First choice. Seek first God's kingdom." I invite God to open my eyes to what He has for me in His Word and read a portion, listening with my heart. I ask Him to guide my thinking, feeling, and doing in the day before me, and I seek His blessing for my family, church, and other requests that are on my heart. Sometimes I sing or listen to worship songs, but every day I seek God's face in His Word. If you're new to the Bible, start with the Gospel of Luke, and then read on through to the end of the New Testament. Then go back and pick up Matthew and Mark. The Old Testament will come later. The point for a spiritual Newborn is to start feeding on God's truth from the Bible by reading the New Testament every day! As you do, the Holy Spirit will help you see your third need as you prepare for the adventures God has in store for you.

A spiritual newborn needs to be changed.

Change Is Healthy—Change Is a Good Thing

A spiritual newborn needs to be changed. I saw this Bible verse posted outside a church nursery, "We shall not all sleep, but we shall all be changed!" (1 Corinthians 15:51 KJV) Parents and caregivers know that physical babies need changing . . . a lot! Pastor Ryan Reed (he and his wife Stacy have recently welcomed their fourth child home) said, "I speak with authority on this subject, and I can tell you that after changing hundreds of diapers, every single one of them stinks!" He went on to say, "I can also tell you that I have never changed one of my babies when they felt ashamed afterward, because the change made them feel fresh and new." Our *Abba* Father also desires that His newborn children feel fresh and new every day. "Anyone who belongs to Christ has become a new person. The old life is gone; a new life has begun!" "And the Lord—who is the Spirit—makes us more and more like him as we are changed into his glorious image" (2 Corinthians 5:17 and 3:18 NLT).

God cleans us up and prepares us to fulfill His purpose and mission in our life. This He does through something the Bible calls *transformation*. Paul challenges us to "be transformed by the renewing of your mind." He continues by explaining the outcome, "Then you will be able to test and approve what God's will is—his good, pleasing and perfect will" (Romans 12:2). God's Spirit will work within us to change the way we think, "renewing" our minds so that we can find and fulfill the will of God. This is how course corrections help us stay on God's mission in life.

Babies are incapable of cleaning themselves up, and parents don't expect them to. Parents clean their children because they love them. In the same way that a newborn child begins a lifetime of physical growth, a newborn believer starts a lifetime journey of spiritual growth, starting with being cleansed, and the cleansing of forgiveness happens, like diaper changes, fairly often!

Believers at all growth stages need God's Spirit to continually cleanse us from all the sinfulness that builds up in our lives and the messes we make as a result. Mature-ish believers understand that we are no more capable of cleaning up those messes ourselves than a newborn is able to change its own diaper. We must be cleansed from all our sins and made right by the substitutionary sacrifice of Christ and the power of God's Spirit alive in us. Salvation is a gift, available only by faith, by which Christ justifies every believer in the eyes of our Heavenly Father. On our own, we can't do anything to earn God's favor.

New believers, however, may need regular reminders not to feel shame about messing up and needing to be cleansed. If we cry out for God's cleansing power as often and as emphatically as a newborn cries to alert a parent that he or she needs changing, God is eager to restore us to a spiritually clean condition. God doesn't want us to suffer from a guilt trip, especially since He is the only one who can take care of the mess anyway. Scripture promises: "If we confess our sins, he is faithful and just and will forgive us our sins and purify us from all unrighteousness" (1 John 1:9). Why is He faithful to forgive us? Because He has already paid the price. It's over. It's done. It's complete. Believe it. Receive it by faith. And thank your *Abba* Father for His promise: "Their sins and lawless acts I will remember no more" (Hebrews 10:17). If God has chosen to forgive and forget our sins, spiritual newborns can believe in God's complete forgiveness. You aren't smarter than God, so agree with what He has said. Jesus is the Lamb of God who takes away your sins. Don't sit in a dirty diaper. Let God clean up your mess and throw it in the garbage. Then you, clean and free, can say, "Thank you, Lord!"

As a new follower of Christ, you don't have to clean up your own act, but as you grow up in the Spirit, you need to let your thinking be renewed and transformed. This means being teachable and responsive to God's Spirit as He makes you aware of areas in your life He desires to make new. Peter provides some concrete next steps in how to navigate this major transformation. He wrote: "Get rid of all evil behavior. Be done with all deceit, hypocrisy, jealousy, and all unkind speech" (1 Peter 2:1 NLT). Such behaviors have no place in the kingdom of God . . . or in the life of a well-loved child.

As a new and growing believer, soon enough you'll learn to go longer periods of time between the stinking messes of your life. You'll begin to abandon the old, harmful habits that keep creating problems: lying, two-faced living, envy, harsh words, and more. For practical insight in learning this kingdom lifestyle, I recommend you to my book, Upside Down Kingdom, as a tool for your personal growth.

Change at Every Stage

Newborns need to let themselves be changed! But so do growing disciples at every stage of their development. Spiritual adults, parents, grandparents, and godparents need to know how to stay clean and help others do the same. Every disciple needs to know how to live a teachable life, receiving God's care and course corrections, then aligning and adjusting to stay on mission with God. Learning the lessons here will accelerate your progress in every stage of your spiritual development. Change is a good thing!

Change is a good thing!

Tiny, helpless newborns don't stay that way very long. They get larger and stronger each day—at an average of an inch in height and 1½ to 2 pounds in weight for each of the first three months. Such rapid growth always seems to surprise new parents, but if you really want to be impressed, consider the growth of a newborn giraffe.

Mama and baby giraffe don't enjoy the sterility of a hospital room or the comfort of a pillow-lined bed. No, the newborn giraffe begins its life by plunging six feet to the ground at the moment of birth, but within ten minutes, it's able to stand up and walk. And within ten hours, it can run at full speed alongside its mother.

In the same way, newborn Christians require the intentional care of mature "parents in the faith" to help them grow into spiritual adulthood. Newborns need others to feed them, and there's nothing wrong with that. However, the newborn stage doesn't need to last very long. You may be a spiritual newborn, but I encourage you to be a "giraffe Christian" in terms of spiritual growth. Now that you're a new creation in God's sight, start running with Him. Don't wait for others to tell you it's okay. Get up! Run! Grow!

Some of the most on-fire Christians I've ever known had only recently come to faith within days or weeks. We tend to think in terms of needing to be a certain age before we're entitled to certain privileges: driving, voting, enlisting in the military, and so forth. But the privilege of growing in God's grace and truth has no age limit. The rate of growth is up to the individual and God. You need not be stalled in the infant stage any longer than you want to be.

Is Perfection My Goal?

Before we close this chapter, there's one other topic that needs our attention. In the Sermon on the Mount, Jesus concludes one section by saying, "Be perfect . . . as your heavenly father is perfect" (Matthew 5:48). This verse troubled me a lot through the years. Is Jesus expecting me to be sinless? Without flaw or mistake in the things I say and do? In the thoughts I think? As a new believer, I transferred my understanding of perfectionism onto Jesus' words and wound up being very judgmental of myself and others. When Jesus said "Judge not, lest you be judged," (Matthew 7:1), my perfectionism rose off the charts! I needed a major course correction. Perfectionism is a recipe for neurosis, judgmentalism, and hypocrisy.

Imagine how relieved I was when a pastor and mentor helped me understand the meaning of the word in its original context. The word *perfect* means "fully mature." Jesus was challenging His listeners to begin with the end in mind . . . to aim high and reach God's intended end goal for us . . . to grow up into our full redemptive potential. One Greek scholar says, "It is well-illustrated with the old pirate's telescope unfolding (extending out) one stage at a time to function at full-strength (capacity, effectiveness)."[4]

Jesus is teaching that human lives are to extend in maturity until they are at full capacity in their effectiveness for God . . . what Paul would call "mature, attaining to the whole measure of the fullness of

Christ" (Ephesians 4:13). *Abba* Father wants every one of His newborns to grow through every stage of their growth. And the good news is that just as a healthy baby is born with all the equipment needed to function as a responsible reproducing adult when developed, you have been born spiritually with all the raw potential and provisions you need to become mature-ish in Christ.

Growing Together

If you feel you are further along in your journey and not so newborn anymore, may I challenge you to make yourself available to help others in their growth? Barnabas helped Saul who would later become Paul. Paul helped Timothy, Titus, Silas, and many others. Ken Dodson, Leila Wilson, and Jim Meek were some of the first people to help me. Later would come Loy Reed and Dr. Boo Heflin. Who can you help to be loved, fed, and changed for the glory of God?

If you are a newborn in God's family, this is a lot to take in, but it will soon begin to make sense. You're starting new habits that will last a lifetime. We never outgrow the need to be fed, cleaned, and loved, do we? The same needs from birth continue throughout our whole lives.

So, continue to feed yourself on every word of God, finding regular nourishment in Scripture. Stay clean by keeping your mind, body, and spirit healthy. Be assured beyond any doubt that you are loved unconditionally. God knows you will make mistakes along the way—just like every other person who has ever lived, except one—so when you do, go to Him quickly for forgiveness and renewal. And don't be shy about asking for help from your new family of believers who are eager to see you grow.

Your next growth stage will be here before you know it.

STAGE	LESSON
Godparent	
Grandparent	
Parent	
Adult	
Adolescent	
Preteen	
Child	
Toddler	
Infant	
Newborn	Be born again and receive God's wonderful new life.

At the end of each chapter, you'll find some questions to stimulate reflection, and hopefully, conversation with others who are on the journey with you. Don't rush through these. Take the time to think, pray, discuss them, and trust God to help you grow.

ADVENTURE PAGES

Pilot's Flight Plan

1. What do you recall about your Newborn stage of spiritual growth? How did you become a believer in the first place?

2. Why is a newborn drinking milk an appropriate metaphor for a new believer reading Scripture?

   What's the difference between Scripture being "milk" for some people, and "solid food" for others? (See 1 Corinthians 3:1-3.)

3. What were/are the habits in your life that require(d) you to seek God's cleansing?

   How do you try to remain clean after God cleanses you?

4. What connections have you discovered between your love for God and your amount of love for fellow believers?

5. What kind of Christian "family" do you currently belong to? How do they support you in your desire to grow spiritually?

Course Correction

If you only do one thing, do this: Find a Bible that's easy to read and begin reading Luke. If it's only five minutes every day, start there.

Captain's Log

If you're helping a new believer grow, I suggest:

➤ Spend time together, and at least some of the time, without a specific agenda. Take the new believer with you every chance you get—to church, to sporting events, shopping, and anywhere else. Your loving presence means more than you can know.

➤ Read the Bible together, just a short passage, maybe from the Gospels, and talk about what each of you observe in the text.

➤ Pray together. Make connecting with God in prayer as natural and normal as your conversations with each other.

MORE TLC, PLEASE!

INFANT

"The hand that rocks the cradle rules the world."

—Glen Campbell

David Ring is a national evangelist and motivational speaker who has cerebral palsy. David and I were in college together, and since then, I've worked with him, traveled with him, and heard him speak more times than I can remember. Of the many memorable lines I've heard him say, this one rings so true: "Everybody needs a mama's love." Physical little ones do. Spiritual children do, too.

Love, though, isn't just being sentimental. It's strong! If grizzly bears had lived in Palestine, Jesus may have said something like this: "O Jerusalem, Jerusalem! How often I have longed to gather your children together as a mama grizzly ferociously and tenderly protects and defends her cubs, but you were not willing." Of course, I know Luke quotes Jesus saying, "how often I have longed to gather your children together, as a hen gathers her chicks under her wings" (Luke 13:34). As a twenty-first-century city dweller, the image of a mother hen sounded kind of lame and weak to me, but then I found out that hens are tender with their chicks, yet become fiercely defensive when danger is on the prowl. I now believe Jesus was harnessing language that everyone in His culture would understand as powerfully protective, and had no intention of suggesting weakness. You don't mess with mama hen's chicks! If you think I'm exaggerating, you can see for yourself on YouTube. In one video a hen takes on an attacking cobra—squawking and using her wings and beak to fight it off. She defends and delivers each of her little chicks to safety. I've never seen such an attack chicken! She was crazy in the fight, placing herself in harm's way to see that every one of her chicks was safe.[5]

I'm thinking Jesus had something like that in mind, similar to God's promise recorded by Isaiah the prophet: "As a mother comforts her child, so will I comfort you; and you will be comforted over Jerusalem" (Isaiah 66:13). Jesus was offering the powerful and personal comfort of God to the people of Jerusalem—covering them, defending them, squawking, flapping, attacking the predators, and protecting them as spiritual children to the point of sacrificing himself for them.

A few years ago, after a fire devastated Yellowstone National Park, a forest ranger hiked into the burned area to inspect the damage. He noticed a bird next to a tree. Both the tree and the bird were burned to a crisp. Yet when he tapped the bird with a stick, three chicks scampered out from under their mother's wings. As the fire approached, she could have flown to safety, but she stayed. She gave her life to protect the little ones she loved.[6]

The Bible introduces God to us in male terms and so we typically think of God as male: "God the Father" and "God the Son." But as we've seen in Isaiah and heard from Jesus, God loves us with the ferocity and tenderness of a mother. This becomes especially meaningful when it comes to the stage of spiritual growth called Infant. In Paul's first letter to the church in the Greek town of Thessalonica, he wrote: "Just as a nursing mother cares for her children, so we cared for you. Because we loved you so much, we were delighted to share with you not only the gospel of God but our lives as well" (1 Thessalonians 2:7-8). The word translated "mother" here was used to communicate the deepest level of tender loving care.

Think of a nursing mother cherishing her child in her arms. That's the picture Paul paints for how spiritual parents help God's Newborns become Infants and Toddlers . . . and eventually, Adults. He says he loves them in a tenderly personal and self-giving way . . . like a nursing mother!

This brings to mind another amazing promise from God in Isaiah: "Can a mother forget the baby at her breast and have no compassion on the child she has borne? Though she may forget, I will not forget you! See, I have engraved you on the palms of my hands" (Isaiah 49:15-16). As an expert in the Hebrew Scriptures, Paul may have had that thought in mind when he declared his tender affection and devotion to the growing new believers in Greece.

"Everybody needs a mama's love."

TLC is what we're talking about here. Tender Loving Care. It's what we have in mind when we say, "Everybody needs a mama's love." It's the kind of love willing to set aside convention and reputation and demonstrate costly sacrifice as evidence of its depth. In the story of the Prodigal Son, Jesus offers such an image of the father. As the younger son made his way home, hungry and humbled, Jesus describes the scene: "While he was still a long way off, his father saw him and was filled with compassion for him; he ran to his son, threw his arms round him and kissed him" (Luke 15:20). In that culture, it was considered less than respectful, out of character, and even laughable for a grown man to run in public. To do so, he would have had to "gird up his loins," that is, pull his robe or tunic up between his legs, tuck them in at his waist (imagine the look of a big diaper), and then scamper with bare legs.

In the Near East, it was humiliating and shameful for a man to show his bare legs. Yet here, Jesus tells us, the father is so eager to welcome his son that he threw convention to the wind, making himself the object of scandal. And when the father meets his son, he throws his arms around him and kisses him. Here's a father that loves like a mother. Imagine God loving you like that, and you will be fully aligned to Jesus' course corrections in your thinking. God is not the ogre in the sky, the Darth Vader you dread putting you in a chokehold until you pass out. God truly cares for you with God-sized TLC . . . and every spiritual infant needs to let Him! Believe it. Receive it. And share it with others.

What's a Mother Worth?

Motherhood has taken its hits as an institution through the years, but without mothers, none of us would be here. And if that weren't enough to declare a mother's value, a *Forbes* magazine article referenced an interesting survey by Salary.com. For ten years, the website had annually projected how much stay-at-home moms deserved if they could charge for their work. After surveying almost 7,000 mothers, their duties had been broken down into ten categories: CEO, psychologist, cook, daycare center teacher, housekeeper, laundry machine operator, computer operator, facilities manager, janitor, and van driver. (And you complain about *your* workday!) The 2018 survey said Mom's salary should be . . . are you ready for this? . . . $162,581.

When I went back to verify the statistics for this book, the 2019 update had been completed. It listed no fewer than thirty duties in the hybrid job description of "Mom," adding such tasks as network administrator, social media communications, and recreational therapist. The additional duties and current economy had warranted a 9.6 percent increase, bringing the latest estimated median annual salary for stay-at-home moms to $178,201.[7] And that was before COVID, by the way. During the pandemic, stay-at-home moms have put in more hours than ever because now, in addition to their own work, they must also be teachers and try to keep the kids from bothering a spouse who's working from home.

My point is not only to highlight the often-overlooked value of the work mothers do, but to underline the truth that spiritual infants need a mother's quality of love, a fierce and tender loving care in order for children to grow healthy and strong.

Long-term Impact

Many studies have shown the importance of nurture in the early years of a child's development. We know this is true instinctively because we've seen the dramatic contrast: the damage caused when children don't feel safe and adored, and the stability, confidence, and creativity of those who do. In other words, how we start matters in the long run . . . it matters a lot!

In an article in *Psychology Today*, Dr. Darcia Narvaez observes that "as the infant's needs are met, the neuronal architecture of the brain and neurobiological systems are supported as they are developing rapidly, enabling proper functioning. At a very basic level, babies are self-actualizing when their needs are met—they are getting support to follow the inner guidance system that Maslow found so important for self-actualization to occur." She explains the impact that shows up later in life: "Adults who received nurturing and responsive care environments in their early years demonstrate greater resilience to stressful situations, better immune functioning, less anxiety and overall, fewer physical health problems."[8]

We can make a similar observation about how people begin their spiritual lives. God doesn't intend for young believers to be left on their own to figure things out. Isolation can happen in big crowds, and it takes more than large worship services to nurture those who are new to the faith. If you're at this stage, be sure to find people who will be involved in your growth and encourage you to absorb God's truth. And if you know someone who is at this stage, don't take anything for granted! Help them feel loved and valued and wanted and connected. The earliest months of spiritual life remind me of the old adage, "As the twig is bent, so grows the tree."

Learning to Crawl

We're newborns only for the first two or three months of our lives—a period when we're helpless and everything must be done for us. Then, for the balance of the first year, we're classified as *infants*. We're still tremendously dependent on others, of course, yet our senses start taking in all sorts of information—sights, sounds, smells, tastes, feelings—and we try to sort out what's most essential. Vision begins to focus, and as it does, we instinctively reach toward objects that capture our attention. We become ambulatory, first crawling and eventually celebrating the ability to stand upright. We realize that people communicate through sound, and we try to separate random noises from the messages our parents and siblings communicate, which we somehow know we need to decode.

Loving parents try to foster growth in all these areas. They connect audibly through calm and assuring speech, praise, reading, and singing. They relate visually with smiles and colorful toys. They use touch to cuddle their little ones.

Parents also realize the need for extreme caution at this age. When a baby is a newborn, he or she doesn't go anywhere or do anything outside the parent's reach. Now, however, it doesn't take long for an inquisitive infant to crawl to a precarious position at the top of the stairs for a better view, to reach for any number of interesting-looking objects to put in his mouth, or to step face first into a sharp corner of a table while learning to walk. Responsible parents take great pains to "baby proof" their homes. We move the breakables to a higher shelf. We start padding the corners of any table that's within range. We put safety plugs in every electrical outlet in the house. And even then, an energetic infant can find potential threats the parent could never anticipate. At the Infant stage, the world is an enormous and incredible place, but it can also be dangerous.

Spiritual Infancy

In this book, we're taking a close look at the continuum of growth that believers experience as we become spiritually mature-ish. Remember, as in the physical so also the spiritual—progress follows a process.

The New Testament says that every believer begins the journey toward maturity by becoming a spiritual newborn. At that point, growth begins immediately by feeding on the milk of God's Word. Paul uses the image of a nursing mother (1 Thessalonians 2:7-8).

When babies are little, they need help to stay fed, to stay clean, and to receive the love and family support they need. This is true throughout the Newborn, Infant, and Toddler (the "Feed me!") stages. Spiritually speaking, we stay fed through God's Word—the Bible. As we get into the Word, the Word gets into us and our souls are fed. We stay clean through prayer and confession. The Holy Spirit puts His finger on what needs to be changed and then assures us of God's forgiveness. And we find abundant love in a fellowship of believers as we share our lives with our new family.

Spiritual Parenting

Just as mothers lead the way in our biological, emotional, and social development, so also *spiritual* mothers (and fathers and leaders and teachers and mentors and grandparents, all who love us like mothers) help us develop spiritually.

Can you think of someone who gave you God-sized tender loving care during your early Christian life? The person can be male or female, but as Paul says he loved like a mother, each of us also need TLC to grow. God used Leila Wilson in my life. Leila was an eighty-one-year-old shut-in, but she was God's chosen instrument to help me early in my developing spiritual life. She was a retired missionary from the Philippines, and I met her while visiting seniors with a pastor. Before we left the little trailer she called home, God moved my heart as she prayed, "Lord, don't put me on the shelf. Use me as it pleases You." The Lord prompted me to ask if she would be willing to teach me and a group of my friends in a summer Bible study. She said, "Yes." And for the remaining weeks of the summer, a group of long-haired, newly saved teenagers were eating our way through 1 Corinthians under a former missionary who looked like Corrie Ten Boom. I will forever thank God for Leila's T&TLC. What's that? Tough and Tender Loving Care!

Jim Meek, a Christ-following upperclassman at Arizona State University was another mentor for me. I noticed a special light in his eyes. He was on fire for God! I wanted what he had, so I hung out with him and learned how he followed Jesus, what Bible he used, how he had his daily time with God, and how he "walked in the Spirit."

Ken Dodson was another. He was a pastor who looked like a prophet and preached like he had something to say that I needed to hear! I met him when his daughter caught me climbing through a window trying to get into the worship center of the First Baptist Church in Winslow, Arizona. I was halfway in when I heard a voice say, "May I help you, young man?" I climbed out and explained that as I walked by, I remembered Jesus saying, "My house is a house of prayer." However, when I found the doors were locked, I had found a window that wasn't and was going in to pray.

Ken asked if I would pray with him, and so began a wonderful relationship with a true mentor in the Spirit. There have been others through the years who have helped me grow in each stage of development, but I've never forgotten the lessons I learned during those early years of my spiritual journey about the ferocity and devotion of godly TLC. The impact of these people has given me the staying power of my life and ministry over the years.

Peter challenged the young church: "Now that you have purified yourselves by obeying the truth so that you have sincere love for each other, love one another deeply, from the heart" (1 Peter 1:22). He's talking about love at its full intensity, like a mother for her child. Literally, the words he chooses mean "to stretch out fully," "to cover," "to go all out to love one another." Demonstrate love like a mother hen or a mama grizzly, and like the mother bird in the Yellowstone fire.

A mother's love: Jesus exemplifies it, and Isaiah, Paul, and Peter write about it. The love that they describe is the kind of love that provides TLC when we most need it—while we're first establishing a growing relationship with our loving Father. And God wants His spiritual children to experience that love to the fullest.

Growing through Spiritual Infancy

When parents have a child—especially their first child—they're often very concerned that its growth is "normal." They consult books and charts and doctors to see what's supposed to happen and when, and they tend to panic if their infant fails to hit one of those milestones. "My child is almost a year old, but he isn't walking yet. What's wrong with him, doctor?" "Our next-door neighbor's daughter is already eating cereal on her own, but ours doesn't know which end of the spoon to hold." Worried parents find dozens of things to obsess about, but those benchmarks are only guidelines based on averages. No two babies are alike, and any two infants may have quite a different pace when it comes to crawling, rolling over, laughing, grasping objects, saying "Mama," or whatever.

The same is true when we consider the spiritual growth of new believers at the Infant stage. Early growth is so continuous and so natural that it can be hard to gauge. When you begin to learn how to hear God's Word and apply it, the Bible tells us that you're taking your first steps of faith. When you speak your first words in prayer, talking to God, you know you're on the right track in learning how to pray. But it's less clear to determine when you've moved from Newborn to Infant, and then from Infant to Toddler.

At these early stages, don't be too concerned with where you are on the chart. Just keep growing. You'll see progress soon enough that you've moved from one stage to the next. Besides, regardless of the progress of the child, the mother will still respond to its cry.

In one study, researchers recorded four minutes of crying from twenty infants, recorded while their parents were out of the room. They pulled six fifteen-second segments from each tape and later had parents listen to a series of twenty-four segments: a random assortment that included six clips of their own infant and eighteen from other infants. The parents averaged 5.5 out of 6 in identifying their own child, although there were a few false positives along the way. Dads had an accuracy of forty-five percent, but moms were correct eighty percent of the time.[9] (Hmmm. Who knew?)

Other studies show that a mother not only recognizes the cry of her child; she knows how to interpret it. Both infants and toddlers tend to cry easily and often, and to casual listeners the cries sound alike. But a loving mother knows better. She can tell that sometimes the cry means "I'm lonely; come get me." Sometimes the cry means "I'm dirty; come change me." Sometimes it means "I'm hurt; come help me." Sometimes it communicates "I'm mad; can you feel me?" To a mother, each cry is precious; it's a clear request for attention and care.

On a spiritual level, every cry is precious to God, and we may cry out to God for many different reasons. As a newborn Christian, your primary emotion is typically sheer joy as you revel in a new and thrilling relationship with the Lord of the universe. Your eyes are opened to God's plan for your life and His attention to meet your needs, and the outlook for your life becomes immediately more hopeful. Yet at the Infant stage, you may find yourself moved with godly sorrow as you continue to feed on God's Word.

As you continue to read Scripture as an infant, you start to come to grips with the price that Jesus paid to provide your new relationship with God. You see that He experienced great suffering, humiliation, and a cruel and painful death to accomplish your salvation. The realization of this horrible truth, especially for someone with a new and tender heart, can move people to tears. Later you may shed tears for other reasons as you cry out to God. Indeed, tears are an appropriate response to many of the emotions and situations we experience throughout our journey toward greater spiritual maturity. Let me give you one of my favorite biblical examples.

A Bottle Full of Tears

Many of the psalms were the equivalent of our worship songs—general expressions of praise or concern that were expressed to God in music. Others, however, were written in response to a specific situation or circumstance the psalmist was going through. For example, Psalm 51 was a prayer of confession after David's adultery with Bathsheba and his murder of her husband had been exposed.

Psalm 56 addressed another specific crisis. David was hiding out in Philistine territory while trying to avoid being killed by King Saul. But he wasn't safe there either. In fact, he was in Gath, the hometown of Goliath, whom he had recently vanquished and slain on the battlefield. Take a look at his emotional state, and his honesty with God:

> O God, have mercy on me, for people are hounding me.
> My foes attack me all day long.
> I am constantly hounded by those who slander me,
>   and many are boldly attacking me.
> But when I am afraid, I will put my trust in you.
> I praise God for what he has promised.
> I trust in God, so why should I be afraid?
> What can mere mortals do to me?
> They are always twisting what I say;
>   they spend their days plotting to harm me.
> They come together to spy on me—
>   watching my every step, eager to kill me.
> Don't let them get away with their wickedness;
>   in your anger, O God, bring them down.
>   (Psalm 56:1-7 NLT)

Can you relate to David's dilemma? He's hiding out in unfriendly territory, but he can't go home because the situation there is even worse! Yet to his credit, he cries out to God for help and direction, and as he does, he realizes a life-changing truth:

> You keep track of all my sorrows.
> You have collected all my tears in your bottle.
> You have recorded each one in your book. (Psalm 56:8 NLT)

This was a dynamic young man God had already anointed to be the next king of Israel. He had gone boldly onto the battlefield and killed the giant Goliath, and he was building his own faithful army of "mighty men." Yet the traumatic events at this stage in David's life were so numerous and severe that they brought him to tears. What did David do? He took his tears to God. So tender and attentive is God that David feels safe taking his tears to Him. He believes that God was perfectly aware of every tear he had ever shed; it was as if He had saved them all in a bottle. Some people collect mugs, stamps or baseball cards. David says God collects our tears.

Some people collect mugs, stamps or baseball cards. David says God collects our tears.

Another insight in this psalm is equally encouraging. David believes that God was also keeping a book about his growth. These days many parents have baby books for each of their children. Mom and Dad record significant dates and events for posterity: birth certificate, baby's first word, date of first steps, photos from first birthday, a lock of hair from the first haircut, a sampling from the abundance of artwork that has you convinced your child is the next Picasso, and other mementos. The book may not seem special to anyone beyond the baby's parents, grandparents, and perhaps a few other relatives. But someday the adult children will find their books and know that they were loved for their entire lives—from birth onward. I will never forget how special I felt when my mother gave me the scrapbook she'd assembled through the years about me. Think of it! God is keeping up with your growth in a book about you!

One helpful way to monitor your spiritual growth is to keep a book of your own—a daily journal. Every day you can take a few minutes to record what you're learning about God, or about yourself in relation to God.

Describe how you're feeling. Write out verses or short passages that are meaningful to you. Include any questions you have about spiritual matters. Then, as months and years pass, you can look back at earlier entries and see how much progress you've made. (You will likely be shocked at your rate of growth!)

You're Still at the Beginning

I hope you don't take offense if you're at this early stage of spiritual growth. Being compared to a crying baby may make you sound helpless. The physical comparisons of crying babies aren't intended to be embarrassing, but no one has a shortcut to maturity. We all start at the beginning. Everyone starts as a Newborn and goes through this Infant stage, but we keep moving onward and upward. Throughout the process of spiritual growth, the point is to embrace your current stage and then grow from there.

However, if all this talk about babies and crying makes you feel a bit juvenile, perhaps you can think in terms of "groans" rather than "cries." Regardless of the stage of spiritual maturity, we all experience times when we find it difficult to connect with God. Perhaps we can't find the words to express our deepest concerns, or we just don't have enough faith to keep asking for what we need. You need to know, that doesn't prevent our loving Lord from knowing exactly what we're crying out for, and in response to our cries, providing us with everything we need. See how Paul explains this divine awareness:

We know that all creation has been groaning as in the pains of childbirth right up to the present time. And we believers also groan, even though we have the Holy Spirit within us as a foretaste of future glory, for we long for our bodies to be released from sin and suffering. We, too, wait with eager hope for the day when God will give us our full rights as his adopted children, including the new bodies he has promised us. We were given this hope when we were saved. . . . And the Holy Spirit helps us in our weakness. For example, we don't know what God wants us to pray for. But the Holy Spirit prays for us with groanings that cannot be expressed in words. And the Father who knows all hearts knows what the Spirit is saying, for the Spirit pleads for us believers in harmony with God's own will. (Romans 8:22-24, 26-27 NLT)

Crying out to God isn't a childish thing to do; it is a human thing.

Crying out to God isn't a childish thing to do; it is a human thing. It's what continues our growing relationship with God. This passage affirms that God doesn't have to hear our desires expressed in words to know what we need from Him. When we find ourselves unable to adequately express ourselves—whether an Infant who is brand new to God's family or a spiritual Grandparent who has been maturing for years—the Holy Spirit steps from within us to take our groanings to the Father on our behalf. We may be unaware of God's presence at times, but He's never unaware of ours.

Experts in child psychology say that parents need to meet a child's basic physical needs. We need to let them know that they are okay. We need to help them feel safe, and to discover and develop their senses. When our little children come to us in tears, they're looking for a safe place to find God-sized tender loving care that will help them persevere through their current crisis.

Progress Involves a Process

We've seen in the previous chapter that newborns need to be loved, fed, and changed. And we've now seen that infants take those needs to a new level, both physically and spiritually. Infants require solid foods, not just milk. As physical dexterity improves, children move from the bottle to a sippy cup, and from the nipple to a spoon. Cleaning shifts from disposable diapers to pull-up training pants to help growing children start learning to take some responsibility to stay clean. No longer needing to be carried everywhere, children now move by rolling and crawling, and eventually getting up and walking on their own.

But with increasing age comes other needs: the need for comfort when in trouble, the need for courage to face fear, the need for consistency to ensure security, and then the need for cultivating self-control. Those major changes are initiated at the spiritual Infant phase, and continue at a new pace as God's spiritual children grow to become Toddlers. A whole new world of adventure is about to open.

At every stage, we need to stay in communication with Mission Control. As we grow, we'll be more perceptive (and quicker) to make mid-course corrections, and the shape of our God-given adventure will become clearer.

STAGE	LESSON
Godparent	
Grandparent	
Parent	
Adult	
Adolescent	
Preteen	
Child	
Toddler	
Infant	Receive nourishing care from your loving heavenly Father and other spiritual "parents" who want to help you grow.
Newborn	Be born again and receive God's wonderful new life.

ADVENTURE PAGES

Pilot's Flight Plan

1. Recall two or three people who "mothered" you with spiritual TLC during different periods in your spiritual journey so far. Specifically, how did each person help you make progress?

2. Have you come across anything in Scripture that has moved you to tears or caused you to feel confusion or sorrow? What was it? Have you discussed it with anyone yet? Why or why not?

3. Consider David's image of God collecting every tear in a bottle and recording each sorrow in a book. What does that say about God? How does that make you feel?

4. Do you keep a spiritual journal? If you do, what benefits are you seeing? If not, how could it help you in your ongoing journey of spiritual growth?

Course Correction

If you do only one thing, do this: find someone who will be a mentor or coach for you. It may be one of the most important connections you've ever made.

Captain's Log

If you're helping someone in this stage grow, I suggest:

➤ Use at least five affirmations for every correction (and shoot for ten to one).

➤ Share the troubles that make you cry or groan. This will normalize inevitable struggles we all experience, and you can explain how God has brought you through . . . eventually.

➤ Many people have experienced difficult family backgrounds and have a hard time believing God really loves them. Consider asking, "How did your parents express their love for you?" And listen. Really listen.

LEARNING TO WALK AND TALK

TODDLER

> "Someday you will be old enough to start reading fairy tales again."
>
> **—C. S. Lewis**

Have you ever heard somebody say, "It's time to walk the walk and talk the talk!"? The stage in our physical development where we typically learn to walk and talk is called Toddler, which has many similarities to the third stage of our spiritual development. At this stage we become more alert and aware of spiritual truths, and we start putting them into words and actions. Don't be embarrassed if you feel like a spiritual toddler. Some very significant life lessons are learned at this level. Learn the lessons of the stage you are in and grow *through* it as you come to know your heavenly Father's pleasure! Remember, progress follows a process.

Learning to Walk with God

Physically, the toddler phase spans ages one through three. It's when youngsters are starting to learn how to walk—falling down, getting up, falling again, getting up again. Muscles are strengthening and balance is developing. It's not uncommon to see a parent and toddler walking hand in hand—not necessarily because the child needs physical support, but because the youngster simply enjoys the added confidence the parent offers, as well as the special feeling of intimacy. Spiritual toddlers too, have a lot of ups and downs as they take their first steps of faith. As they trust God's Word and find His balance in applying the commands of Jesus, their confidence increases and their strides become surer and steadier.

Learning to walk with God can bring some "cool" to your every day.

In the story of creation, God walked in the Garden of Eden in the "cool of the day," regularly communicating with Adam and Eve (Genesis 3:8). In the same way, learning to walk with God can bring some "cool" to your every day. God is like a parent wanting to take steps together with His beloved child. Unfortunately, the sin of Adam and Eve ended that intimate, interpersonal relationship, and we've suffered the difficulty of reconnecting with God ever since. Still, that's the goal of spiritual growth and maturity—increased intimacy with God as we grow to "be filled to the measure of all the fullness of God" (Ephesians 3:19) and learn to "walk in the Spirit" (Galatians 5:16), fulfilling God's mission for our lives.

It's a surprising tidbit of history that astronaut Buzz Aldrin, on his Apollo 11 mission fifty years ago, took Holy Communion on the moon! NASA kept it quiet over concerns of unwanted attention, but Aldrin, the second man to walk on the moon, was a devout believer in Christ and leader at his church. The first thing he did when the Eagle landed was give thanks to God. With special permission from NASA, he had launched into space with bread and wine for communion with God in a special worship moment on the lunar surface. When the moment came, he quoted Jesus saying, "I am the vine, you are the branches. Whoever remains in me, and

I in him, will bear much fruit; for you can do nothing without me" (John 15:5). Buzz trusted that what he was doing in the NASA program was "part of God's eternal plan for man." Talk about walking with God!

Another person we read about in Genesis is a man named Enoch. He was a sixty-five-year-old toddler when he started learning to walk with God. Then, three hundred years later, "Enoch walked faithfully with God; then he was no more, because God took him away" (Gen 5:21-24). An old story is told that God so enjoyed His walks with Enoch that each day they took longer walks together, farther and farther away from where Enoch lived. One day God said, "We're closer to My home today than yours—why don't you just come home with Me?" The New Testament tells us, "By faith Enoch was taken from this life, so that he did not experience death: 'He could not be found, because God had taken him away.' For before he was taken, he was commended as one who pleased God" (Hebrews 11:5).

It pleases God when we learn to walk with Him. Proud and happy parents cheer and clap and post videos of their toddler's first steps so others can celebrate with them, and in the same way, God is pleased when you take your first steps in faith with Him. It has been said, "Every journey begins with a first step."

One of the most popular books Dr. Seuss ever wrote was *Oh, the Places You'll Go!* which inspires people to step out and step up in life. When Viola and Stephen Armstrong witnessed their firstborn son, Neil, take his first steps, they had no idea he would one day be walking on the moon and make one of the most dramatic statements ever spoken: "That's one small step for man, one giant leap for mankind." God wants us to go places with Him, and learning how to walk is the way forward into the adventure.

Going Places with God

There are only two places in the Bible where we read that someone was taken by God rather than dying: Enoch, who walked with God, and the great prophet Elijah who was caught up in a chariot of fire. As for the rest of us, even when we "walk through the valley of the shadow of death," we can do it without fear. Why? Because the Lord, our Shepherd, who's been walking with us through life, will also walk with us through death to the other side (Psalm 23:4).

After the death and resurrection of Jesus, and the coming of the Holy Spirit, believers are again able to walk with God and called to "walk by the Spirit" (Galatians 5:16). In our associations with others, we're called to "walk in the way of love" (Ephesians 5:2). We choose to walk in God's light rather than darkness (1 John 1:6-7).

Let's push the illustration. As much as we enjoy the ability and free-dom to *walk*, we also learn to *run* at the Toddler stage. We like the sensation of speed and feeling the wind in our face and hair. When my youngest daughter, Jess, learned to walk, she immediately also started running . . . on her tiptoes! Everywhere she went, she ran on tiptoes!

Who sets the pace for your walk with God? You do. And spiritually, at this stage we learn that those who trust in the Lord find strength not only to walk and not faint, but also to run without growing weary . . . and even to soar high on wings like eagles (Isaiah 40:31). We begin to view our spiritual growth as a marathon, and we need to train so we can "run with perseverance the race marked out for us" (Hebrews 12:1). We run with purpose, because there's a prize at the end of the race (1 Corinthians 9:24-26). The lessons the Apostle Paul learned from his early steps of walking with Jesus served him to the end of his biological life, when his last words included, "I have fought the good fight, I have finished the race, I have kept the faith. Now there is in store for me the crown of righteousness" (2 Timothy 4:7-8). Walking with God and "running the race" become lifetime commitments. They begin when we're spiritual newborns, of course, but the Toddler stage is the time most of us begin to develop a deeper awareness of their importance and commit ourselves to ongoing spiritual progress . . . or not. How sad would it be if my physical children came to this point in their development and then stopped! It's no less sad when spiritual children don't take steps of faith to keep growing.

Learning to Talk

For the first year of their lives, our children hear us talking and try to figure out what all those sounds mean. After about a year, they begin to discern and repeat the most basic words: *mama, dada, blankie.* My firstborn's first word was "Aight!" I had Corrie in my arms, and she was looking up, naming what she saw overhead: "Light!" By the Toddler stage, children start stringing together syllables to make words, and connecting words to construct sentences. Their vocabulary grows rapidly during this stage, as does their clarity of speech.

Even if you are not new to the Bible, the book can seem a bit daunting . . . if not intimidating. It's thick, over a thousand pages long, and full of names of people and places that sound very strange and hard to pronounce. Not to mention that for many of us, reading isn't the top of our daily Things-to-Do List. Still, spiritual nutrition is absolutely vital for spiritual newborns, infants, and toddlers. But another reason for the daily intake of Scripture is learning the language of your spiritual life and family.

If you are a new and growing believer who is feeding on the truths of Scripture, biblical language may sound strange to you at first. The truths of the Bible are mostly clear and simple. Newborn and infant believers enjoy the familiar Old Testament stories, the accounts of Jesus' life and ministry, the many promises of God, and other portions of Scripture that are easily understood and applied. However, as we continue reading, we will most certainly encounter names and terms that are unfamiliar and challenging. Names like Melchizedek, Zerubbabel, and Jehoshaphat, so mysterious and strange. Sometimes two or more different Bible characters will have the *same* name. For example, one Joseph was the coat-of-many-colors guy in the Old Testament who, after many personal trials, ended up in a high-level position in Egypt and stored enough food to get everyone through a severe seven-year famine. Another Joseph was the husband of Mary, the mother of Jesus. A third was instrumental in the formation of the early church, although he went by his nickname, Barnabas, "Son of Encouragement" (Acts 4:36). You'll also find multiple people named Mary, James, and even Judas. So just as every toddler tries to make sense of adult language, a spiritual toddler should do her best to make sense out of unfamiliar and strange-sounding biblical names. Don't let them scare you away from feeding on God's Word.

A friend of mine from an Italian family told me that when he was a new believer, he read the Bible's table of contents for the very first time and was thrilled to see an Italian in the lineup: Malachi. But rather than the traditional pronunciation of MAL-uh-kai, his Italian eyes saw the name as Ma-LAH-chee! So as you read, don't get snagged on names or pronunciations. Ask the Holy Spirit to help you learn and speak the language of love: "The only thing that counts is faith expressing itself in love" (Galatians 5:6).

In addition to names and places, you will find new words that carry deep meanings of theological truth that God wants to make real in your life. Words like grace, holiness, incarnation, atonement, reconciliation, justification, propitiation, sanctification, and glorification. You don't need to fully understand these concepts at the Toddler stage, but you shouldn't avoid them either. They'll come up again and again throughout your growth stages, and they'll eventually become clearer to you. At this point, I'm just giving fair warning to spiritual toddlers to not be too concerned if you come across passages and concepts in Scripture that sound like they're way over your head. Just keep reading, talking to committed mentors, and moving forward. It's all part of learning the language of the faith.

Talking to God in Prayer

Another very significant way of "faith expressing itself in love" is through praying. Paul tells the new believers in Greece to "pray continually" (1 Thessalonians 5:17). That doesn't mean we have to always have our heads bowed and eyes closed. It means we always keep our conversation with God open and active. To the people of Philippi, he writes, "Don't worry about anything; instead, pray about everything. Tell God what you need, and thank him for all he has done. Then you will experience God's peace, which exceeds anything we can understand. His peace will guard your hearts and minds as you live in Christ Jesus" (Philippians 4:6-7 NLT).

Praying is simply talking with God, so feel free to talk with the Lord as personally as you do to a family member or close friend.

Praying is simply talking with God, so feel free to talk with the Lord as personally as you do to a family member or close friend. Remember, He loves you and loves to hear the sound of your voice. You can pray about anything and everything. Ask God for what you need and thank Him when He answers. Tell Him how much you love Him. Offer your praise and worship for who He is and your gratitude for what He does. He wants us to open our souls and pour our hearts out to Him. He knows what we are going through and, since Jesus was among us as God in the flesh, He knows what it feels like to be human. "We do not have a high priest who is unable to empathize with our weaknesses, but we have one who has been tempted in every way, just as we are—yet he did not sin. Let us then approach God's throne of grace with confidence, so that we may receive mercy and find grace to help us in our time of need" (Hebrews 4:15-16).

Praying is the pipeline by which God brings the flow of His peace and grace into our hearts. It is also a powerful weapon in spiritual battle (more about that when we get to spiritual adolescence). For now, start talking to

God all the time—when you get up in the morning, as you read the Bible to start your day, before each meal, throughout the day as you make decisions, and at night as you lie down to sleep. There is never a wrong time to pray! It's part of talking the talk of your new life in Christ.

Learning Discipline

Personally, as a grandparent of preschoolers, I think toddlers are lots of fun to have around. There's never a dull moment! Toddlers have an inordinate amount of curiosity, which is generally a positive trait. Every definitive statement by an adult is usually met with a "Why?" They're very teachable at this stage, and wise parents will let them express their curiosity in lots of different ways: reading, building, exploring, drawing, painting, music, and other activities.

As their spike in curiosity is peaking, their physical dexterity is improving. Not only can they now run and jump, they're also able to climb stairs and crawl onto structures. They can turn doorknobs and twist open jars. Parents want to give their toddlers every opportunity to learn, but they need to keep a watchful eye open to prevent them from being harmed.

Coupled with the increasing physical capabilities of toddlers is a growing focus on themselves. Yes, during this phase they learn to walk and run, but now they don't always choose to come when you call them. Not long after they learn to talk, they learn to *talk back* to parents. They're developing a will of their own. In addition to "Why?" their favorite words seem to be "No!" and "Mine!" The concept of sharing is foreign to them, and temper tantrums are far too common. Parents quickly learn that this is the phase of the "terrible twos," as the toddler begins to establish his own identity.

It's no easy task for parents of toddlers to simultaneously encourage the child's desire to learn while establishing clear boundaries to prevent her curiosity from getting out of hand. Discipline becomes necessary, and

despite what the child thinks, most parents attempt to see that it's conduct-
ed lovingly, consistently, and fairly. However, if parents are persistently
loving and hold their children accountable, toddlers will eventually learn
that it's much easier to *work with* their parents rather than *resist* them so
strongly.

Spiritual discipline can be confusing for Christian toddlers. The previous stages of Newborn and Infant were times when spiritual parents did
almost everything for them, but now they need to begin to take responsibility for their choices. As we continue to feed on the Word of God,
we're likely to come across certain passages that call for major changes in
our established habits and behaviors—and when the toddler mentality
kicks in, we may resist what we're reading. We demand to know why, or we
stomp our feet and say "No!" Unfortunately, some growing believers tend
to stall out in this defiant "terrible twos" spiritual stage. Some don't like to
be told what to do or how to act. Some remain so focused on themselves
that they stay blind to the rights and needs of others. Some just expect
everything to be easy after committing their lives to Christ, and they're
ready to cash in their chips when they start hearing about the realities of
suffering and sacrifice.

But a loving parent never gives up on a growing child, even though he
or she can be quite difficult. Neither does God desert one of His children
who acts in defiance. It's persistent, continuing love that draws the child
back to the Father and the family of believers. This love, however, may
also require some discipline.

One truth of Scripture that needs to be emphasized at the Toddler
stage is that spiritual discipline is motivated by love. The writer to the
Hebrews explains:

> Have you forgotten the encouraging words God spoke to you as
> his children? He said, "My child, don't make light of the Lord's
> discipline, and don't give up when he corrects you. For the Lord

disciplines those he loves, and he punishes each one he accepts as his child."

As you endure this divine discipline, remember that God is treating you as his own children. Who ever heard of a child who is never disciplined by its father? If God doesn't discipline you as he does all of his children, it means that you are illegitimate and are not really his children at all. Since we respected our earthly fathers who disciplined us, shouldn't we submit even more to the discipline of the Father of our spirits, and live forever?

For our earthly fathers disciplined us for a few years, doing the best they knew how. But God's discipline is always good for us, so that we might share in his holiness. No discipline is enjoyable while it is happening—it's painful! But afterward there will be a peaceful harvest of right living for those who are trained in this way. (Hebrews 12:5-11 NLT)

Just as a loving parent might impose a timeout for a defiant toddler to help her learn to control her emotions and listen to what Mom or Dad told her to do, God may allow His children to undergo occasional unpleasant circumstances for their own good. Godly discipline—like proper parental discipline—is always initiated with love, with the desired result of improved behavior and a more peaceful and fulfilling life for the child.

You may sense God creating boundaries for you and prompting you in the Spirit:

➤ "No, we don't use that language in our Christian family, so try to speak kindly next time."

➤ "No, we don't treat people like that; be more compassionate."

➤ "No, I'm not going to answer that prayer for you. It's not time yet."

Most toddlers hear Mom and Dad saying "no" a lot. And at the spiritual Toddler stage, we tend to hear God say "no" quite frequently, but that doesn't mean God is mad at you. What it means is that He's joining the journey with you and trying to keep you safe as you grow. You're in a curiosity stage and boundaries are appropriate . . . and necessary.

We also need to learn, as soon as possible, that God's disciplines are not always a result of our personal misbehavior. Sometimes, yes, we choose a wrong path or do something we shouldn't, and He tries to steer us back to safety again. But other times, discipline is used to make us stronger—to toughen us up for harder struggles at future stages of spiritual growth. Like a coach or trainer who pushes team members to do more than they thought themselves capable of doing, God uses events of our lives—sometimes very difficult or painful events—as a training exercise to develop our trust in His power and deliverance, and as preparation to help others who may be going through similar trials.

Suffering, like discipline, isn't pleasant, yet in God's hands, it's never without purpose. Indeed, suffering initiates a domino effect of personal and spiritual growth. Paul explained, "We also glory in our sufferings, because we know that suffering produces perseverance; perseverance, character; and character, hope. And hope does not put us to shame, because God's love has been poured out into our hearts through the Holy Spirit, who has been given to us" (Romans 5:3-5).

It's like this: *Suffering* → *Perseverance* → *Character* → *Hope.*

How can we ever develop perseverance if we never suffer? How can we become men and women of Christian character if we don't learn to persevere through the events that trouble us? This is the process that eventually helps us arrive at a consistent, confident belief that God will see us through anything and everything we face. That's a level of Christian hope that only comes with spiritual maturity, and spiritual maturity only increases through a faith-filled response to hard times.

(Future chapters will deal with the importance of self-discipline, but at the Toddler stage, discipline is usually imposed by a loving and caring parent.)

A Growth Plan

Another commonality between a physical toddler and someone in the spiritual Toddler stage is the desire to rush maturity. Children love to dress up in their parents' clothes and clomp around in their big shoes, pretending to be adults already. It's perfectly normal and natural to project yourself into a parent's role.

But as we've seen, there's no shortcut to spiritual growth . . . no bypass or express lane to maturity. We don't get to skip any of the stages, even though the spiritual transitions from Newborn to Infant to Toddler can seem tedious to us. We start to wonder if we're ever going to grow up spiritually. Even though a spiritual toddler has a long way to go and grow, it's still good to get off to an ambitious start. But a word of warning: although we'd all like to achieve new levels of maturity, it rarely happens quickly or easily.

Perhaps you happen to be at the spiritual toddler level, and you're reading this and wondering, *What do I have to do to grow to the next level?* Let me offer three short suggestions to help you "stay" the course:

First, *stay curious.* Try to maintain that wonderful toddler's curiosity throughout your lifetime. Hold on to it. Keep learning. Explore and try new experiences, try obeying Jesus' commands, try walking by faith and going deeper into the truths of Scripture. God doesn't mind our questions, our requests, or even our doubts. In fact, He welcomes them. Jesus invited us, "Ask and it will be given to you; seek and you will find; knock and the door will be opened to you. For everyone who asks receives; the one who seeks finds; and to the one who knocks, the door will be opened" (Matthew 6:7-8).

We can miss out on much of what God reveals about himself simply because we don't bother to give it any thought. Asking questions and meditating on confusing truths is an important way we learn. Keep asking "Why?"—especially when it comes to your faith. "Why did God act in that particular way in that situation?" "Why *didn't* God do something when that happened?" "Why does God keep using such imperfect people to accomplish His will?" You will soon discover that the more answers you find, the more questions you will have. (And spoiler alert: you'll never find *all* the answers you're looking for because much of the faith journey remains a mystery. In my life, that mystery is about more than knowing answers. It is about knowing God!)

So, stay curious, but also *stay real*. Toddlers are intensely honest about their imperfections. They fall down a lot, but they get right back up. And they tell you exactly how they're feeling, whether good or bad.

At the spiritual Toddler stage, you must give yourself permission to fail and to feel. Perfectionism haunts some people in this stage. Don't expect to get everything right the first time every time. And when you don't, don't pretend like you did. God knows you're not perfect—and so do all the rest of us! When you learn to trust God throughout your spiritual growth process, you're able to see every failure as a chance for a do-over . . . a fresh start.

Be honest on those days when your faith isn't as strong as it was the day before. No one has a faith growth chart with an arrow that goes perpetually up and to the right. We all have ups and downs, periods of rapid growth interspersed with cold spells. If you start feeling like your faith may be floundering a bit, be honest about it. Just because you don't feel as confident as you did yesterday doesn't necessarily mean your faith is evaporating. There are any number of reasons why you may feel differently.

When I was a little guy, I loved to wrestle with my dad, and now I wrestle with my grandsons. I like to think that when we are little kids spiritually, God also lets us wrestle with Him. I believe He wants us to enjoy wrestling with circumstances that feel a lot larger than we are. He invites us to wrestle with Him in prayer when we go through situations we don't understand. Sometimes we feel like we're getting a big "No!" from God, and we just want to cry. During such times, we need to cling to our faith that God cherishes us, loves us with a mother's TLC, and wants to comfort us. Even as we wrestle with faith in understanding God's will and ways, He never, ever, wants us to stop believing. We can pray like the man did to Jesus who said, "Lord, I believe; help my unbelief!" (Mark 9:24 NKJV).

It's way too easy to fake faith. When we were very young as toddlers, we learned what we were supposed to say and how we were supposed to act. Now, as physical adults but spiritual toddlers, some believers become impatient and begin to pose as giants of faith (much like a toddler dressing up as an adult) when they're still quite immature. These people can do more harm than good—to themselves and those around them.

It's helpful to have a reliable spiritual mentor with whom you can discuss your feelings. Find someone who is regularly available to you. Choose a good listener—someone who will let you pour out your deepest feelings without a lot of interruptions. But it should also be someone who, after listening carefully, can offer sound advice. Regardless of our position on the spiritual growth chart, we can all benefit from the insight and experience of someone who is a bit farther along on the spiritual journey.

So . . . stay curious. Stay real. And then, with all the authenticity, honesty, and energy you can muster, *stay at it.*

So . . . stay curious. Stay real. And then, with all the authenticity, honesty, and energy you can muster, *stay at it.* Most church services are once a week, but faith is developed day by day. Keep trusting daily. Keep praying daily. Eat daily bread of the Word. Exercise your faith daily.

During my early spiritual childhood, I was so spiritually hungry I couldn't get enough of the Bible. I didn't want somebody else feeding me all the time, so I started reading the Bible for myself every day—many times a day. I took it with me everywhere I went. And when I'd read it and something significant popped out, I underlined or highlighted it on the page. Often I wrote meaningful passages on a card, and then I tried to memorize them.

One particular passage was a tremendous encouragement to me. Jesus said, "Consider carefully what you hear. . . . With the measure you use, it will be measured to you—and even more. Whoever has will be given more; whoever does not have, even what they have will be taken from them'" (Mark 4:24-25).

At the time, I don't think I understood the last part, but I was excited about the first part. When Jesus said the measure I use is the one that will be used on me, it meant I could grow spiritually at the pace I chose. What I heard Jesus saying was that if I go all the way with God, then God will go all the way with me. And if I don't do squat, then I'm in danger of losing what I have. But the pace of my spiritual development, the pace of my growth, was up to me and Jesus. I remember thinking, *If that's how it is and my growth doesn't depend on anyone but me, the Lord, and the measure I use, then I can set my own pace, and God will respond to my faith.*

After years of putting that principle into practice, I want to assure you that it's not only true for me, it's also true for you and every one of us who are determined to grow in our faith. God doesn't just want you to grow; He wants you to grow to the measure of all the fullness of God. His purpose is repeated in Scripture (John 17:13; Romans 15:29; Ephesians 3:17-19; 4:16-19).

The measure you use is the measure God uses back with you. We love Him because He first loved us, and He gives us a chance to respond in faith.

If you feel like you're a spiritual toddler, what can you do? Embrace your stage and grow there! Learn to walk (and maybe even start running) in faith. Begin to develop spiritual disciplines. Stay curious, stay real, and stay at it. And one more crucial point: *Don't stay where you are*!

Before you know it, you'll not only be talking the talk, but you'll be walking the walk with joy and confidence and experiencing a deeper, closer walk with God. Earlier I mentioned Buzz Aldrin and his time of worship in taking communion on the moon. At the end of the Apollo 11 mission, as the three astronauts were returning to earth, Aldrin read aloud these words "When I consider thy heavens, the work of thy fingers, the moon and the stars, which thou hast ordained; What is man, that thou art mindful of him? and the Son of Man, that thou visitest him?" (Psalm 8:3-4 KJV) My grandmother's favorite hymn included the words, "He walks with me and He talks with me, and He tells me I am His own." May you know the joy and wonder of walking and talking with God and feeling Him say to you how special you are to Him as you grow on to the next level.

In the first three stages of spiritual development, young believers are saying "feed me." They depend on others to give them the sustenance that helps them grow. Now they're ready for the next three stages. In these, they're saying, "equip me" for great future.

STAGE	LESSON
Godparent	
Grandparent	
Parent	
Adult	
Adolescent	
Preteen	
Child	

Toddler	Learn to walk in faith and talk to God in prayer as you grow in community with God and others.
Infant	Receive nourishing care from your loving heavenly Father and other spiritual "parents" who want to help you grow.
Newborn	Be born again and receive God's wonderful new life.

ADVENTURE PAGES

Pilot's Flight Plan

1. On a scale of one (least) to 10 (most), how would you evaluate your current walk with God? Explain your answer.

   (Are you keeping in step with the Spirit? Do you walk in the way of love? Do you walk in light rather than darkness?)

2. What dangers might spiritual toddlers get into, now that they're capable of walking where they want to go rather than where the parent takes them?

3. What difficult or challenging Scriptures have you found recently in your Bible reading? To what extent are you bothered when you come across lengthy names or unfamiliar concepts?

4. Have you ever felt that God is disciplining you? If so, how did it make you feel? Do you understand that these disciplines are signs of God's love for you? Why is it essential to understand (if not appreciate) God's purpose for discipline?

5. What do you most need to do at this stage of your spiritual journey:
   - ➤ Stay curious?
   - ➤ Stay real?
   - ➤ Or stay at it?

   Explain your response.

Course Correction

If you only do one thing, do this: As you read the Bible, stay curious. In each passage, ask who, what, when, where, how, and why. You'll be surprised how much you notice!

Captain's Log

If you're helping a spiritual toddler grow, I suggest:

➤ As you read the Bible with your friend, point out amazing things and ask great questions.

➤ Take your friend with you to serve.

➤ Celebrate every question he or she asks.

"LOOK WHAT I CAN DO!"

CHILD

*"Look at the skies, they have stars in their eyes
On this lovely bella notte . . ."*

—From the song "Bella Notte," Disney's
Lady and the Tramp

Oh, my. Barely seven years old, coal-black hair in curls draped around her shoulders, wearing a beautiful sleeveless white taffeta holiday dress, she slowly walked her way to the center of the platform at the close of our Christmas Eve worship. Hundreds of us were gathered in the room with unlit candles in hand as we prepared to pass the flame, wick to wick, candle to candle, then lift our lights together to defy the darkness of the room. Twinkle-lights were sparkling like a starry sky overhead and the adult singers surrounding her in the background seemed like an angelic host. Then suddenly . . .

> This little light of mine, I'm gonna let it shine.
> This little light of mine, I'm gonna let it shine.
> This little light of mine, I'm gonna let it shine.
> Let it shine, let it shine, let it shine.

Sophia wasn't breathless, but many of us grownups in the room were! We were so proud and amazed, as one of our young ladies in the making stepped up and stepped out and sang her solo, perfectly in key, full of strength and heart. It was a priceless moment. And Sophia was, in fact, demonstrating the very truth she was declaring, incarnating the words she sang for all to see and hear. Spontaneously, more began joining in, the adult singers and all of us! Her enthusiasm was contagious. Soon the room was illuminated with the soft glow of dancing candlelight.

Move with me now to another Christmas scene. My oldest grandson West, five at the time, has opened one of the gifts under the tree with his name on it: a do-it-yourself kit full of parts waiting to be put together. What would he build? Would it be the fort depicted on the box big enough for him to crawl inside? No, but in a flash, gift wrapping all around, the box is open and parts are coming together as a very determined young engineer is busy building a rocket ship, which he will soon pilot into outer space right from the comfort of the living room!

"This Little Light of Mine" and a do-it-yourself kit. What do they have in common? Enthusiasm and determination are two of the primary qualities of childhood, both biological and spiritual. Biological childhood is a season of, "Watch me! Look at me! Hey Daddy, Mommy, look what I can do!" It's a time when kids thrill to hear grownups say things like, "I know you can do it, and I really believe you can do it on your own." Determination kicks in as children experience the freedom and accomplishment of feeding themselves, dressing themselves, tying their own shoes, taking out the trash, feeding the dog, and trying new games. As they build confidence with newfound enthusiasm and determination, this is a season of rapid growth, and those qualities will be helpful throughout their lifetimes.

The Darkness Will Not Overcome It

In fact, "This Little Light of Mine" is an ideal example. The young child who is joyously singing has little idea of the extent of darkness in the world and the importance of the light. It surprises many people to discover that the song was written in 1920 by music teacher and composer Harry Dixon Loes to be used in Sunday school. Later, the song was adopted and adapted in the 1950s and 1960s to become one of the most popular songs of the Civil Rights Movement, and many people presumed, incorrectly, that it was a traditional Black spiritual.[10]

In addition to its use in the struggle for civil rights, "This Little Light of Mine" has been used much more recently as a unifying song of hope and healing. David Letterman asked folk singer Odetta to be the first artist to perform on his *Late Night* show when it came back on the air after terrorist attacks destroyed the World Trade Centers on September 11, 2001. She led the Boys Choir of Harlem in three songs, one of which was "This Little Light of Mine."[11] An interfaith group sang the song together in Charlottesville, Virginia, in August, 2010, as they protested a "Unite the Right" rally of armed Klansmen and other white nationalists. And the new Mississippi Civil Rights Museum in Jackson includes a dazzling sculpture as a centerpiece where visitors view the history of the movement immersed in the sound of many voices singing "This Little Light of Mine."[12]

So, the next time you see young children—especially your children or grandchildren—singing "This Little Light of Mine" or some other kids' praise song, keep in mind that you never know how a simple song might influence them in years to come. As they mature, they will see more clearly the importance of letting their lights shine in the darkness.

This is just one example of the importance of a lifetime commitment to spiritual maturity. We learn new things about God and ourselves at each stage along the way. Those lessons might not seem relevant right away, but they often turn out to be more essential to our wellbeing than we could ever imagine.

"This Little Light of Mine" was based on one of Jesus' primary emphases in His Sermon on the Mount: "You are the light of the world. A town built on a hill cannot be hidden. Neither do people light a lamp and put it under a bowl. Instead they put it on its stand, and it gives light to everyone in the house. In the same way, let your light shine before others, that they may see your good deeds and glorify your Father in heaven" (Matthew 5:14-16).

Spiritual childhood is when we discover that our words and actions can help others come to know our Father in heaven. Spiritual children are saying, "Watch me. Look at me!" They're taking the initiative, showing confidence and determination so other people can find their way to the light. And their enthusiasm builds as they discover their joy intensifying: first they experience the thrill of serving Jesus, and then they discover that their good deeds may also light the way for others to discover the goodness of God. (However, spiritual children may also arrive at some misperceptions about good works. More on that in a moment.)

We might first learn that great truth of Scripture in a singalong, but the truth becomes more heartfelt as we go along our journey. The song that many of us learn as a perky little children's tune takes on a new significance: it becomes an anthem as we mature and discover the extent and intensity of the moral and spiritual darkness we face from time to time.

An Unforgettable Life Lesson

I particularly like the Gospel account where a child is crucial to the story but is hardly noticed. After Jesus demonstrated the amazing healing power of God, great crowds began to follow Him wherever He went. Imagine today if someone showed up with an effective, instantaneous cure for COVID-19, cancer, MS, or another not-yet-curable disease. Do you suppose he would be popular? Well, Jesus was the healer of all diseases, and the people following Him swelled into thousands. After a long day of teaching and healing, Jesus realized His listeners were hungry. It's as if He was thinking, "You know, people shouldn't only find healing in Me, they should also receive nourishment," so He challenged His disciples to feed the crowd before they went home for the evening. All four Gospels contain this story, but I like John's account:

> When Jesus looked up and saw a great crowd coming toward him, he said to Philip, "Where shall we buy bread for these people to eat?" He asked this only to test him, for he already had in mind what he was going to do.
>
> Philip answered him, "It would take more than half a year's wages to buy enough bread for each one to have a bite!"
>
> Another of his disciples, Andrew, Simon Peter's brother, spoke up, "Here is a boy with five small barley loaves and two small fish, but how far will they go among so many?"
>
> Jesus said, "Have the people sit down." There was plenty of grass in that place, and they sat down (about five thousand men were there). Jesus then took the loaves, gave thanks, and distributed to those who were seated as much as they wanted. He did the same with the fish.
>
> When they had all had enough to eat, he said to his disciples, "Gather the pieces that are left over. Let nothing be wasted." So they gathered them and filled twelve baskets with the pieces of the five barley loaves left over by those who had eaten. (John 6:5-13)

Only John mentions the young boy in the story. The adult disciples appeared helpless and useless. Philip did some mental math to arrive at a quick cost analysis to determine the total expense of feeding everybody. Andrew set out to take a food inventory. They all protested Jesus' instructions, backed with facts and figures. That's what adults do, right? But it was a child who let his little light shine by offering his lunch to Jesus.

Can you imagine that little boy as a grown man, looking back on that day and telling his children and grandchildren about it? I wonder how many times throughout the rest of his life he got to retell the story about the food that just kept coming from his meager lunch, how many people it fed, and all the leftovers! He had let his little light shine, and he saw the good Jesus did with it . . . the good that he and Jesus did together to help so many people and make such a difference in their world. How could that child ever know that we would still be talking today about how he shared his lunch, and what Jesus did with it?

Developing as a spiritual child is like that for all of us. First we learn to let our lights shine for Christ, and then we begin to see the good in the world that results. But like the boy in the story, we aren't likely to ever realize *all* the good that results.

Jesus and Children

Jesus believed childhood is special, and He showed that children deserve our respect. Today, many parents are preoccupied with the stresses of life. They were bad enough before the pandemic, economic disruption, and racial unrest, and now they've doubled! Sometimes, children can feel ignored, or even emotionally abandoned, in the crush of unrelieved pressures on a family. Their parents don't mean to harm their kids, but they feel overwhelmed. Jesus knew something about pressure—He was carrying the weight of the whole world on His shoulders, yet we have no record of Jesus ever saying anything improper because He was under pressure. Jesus always valued children very highly.

The boy with the loaves and fishes was completely overlooked in the accounts of Matthew, Mark, and Luke, and John barely gives him a mention. But almost everywhere else where Scripture describes an encounter between Jesus and a child, an important lesson emerges. Consider these . . .

We know that the disciples frequently bickered among themselves about which of them was the greatest (Matthew 20:20-24; Mark 9:33-34; Luke 9:46; 22:24). One day they came right out and asked Jesus, but they weren't prepared for His answer:

At that time the disciples came to Jesus and asked, "Who, then, is the greatest in the kingdom of heaven?" He called a little child to him, and placed the child among them. And he said, "Truly I tell you, unless you change and become like little children, you will never enter the kingdom of heaven. Therefore, whoever takes the lowly position of this child is the greatest in the kingdom of heaven. And whoever welcomes one such child in my name welcomes me." (Matthew 18:1-5)

What was it about children, exactly, that Jesus admired so much? Clearly, many things we do in our physical childhoods aren't remotely admirable. We bully smaller kids to get our way. We call others mean names. We fight with siblings. We break things and try to hide the evidence, hoping our crime will never be discovered. We're learning to share, but we're not always eager to do it. That's why Paul wrote, "When I was a child, I talked like a child, I thought like a child, I reasoned like a child. When I became a man, I put the ways of childhood behind me" (1 Corinthians 13:11). What did Jesus see in children that Paul didn't? Is there a conflict here? No, not at all.

There's a world of difference between being *childish* and being *childlike*.

There's a world of difference between being *childish* and being *childlike*. Paul's reference was to the childish ways of self-centeredness, jealousy, whining, and greed. As we mature, we need to leave such things behind. But I think Jesus saw the best in children: their willingness to try new things, their joy of discovery, and their simple, unquestioning faith in those who loved them. If we "outgrow" these childlike qualities, it's to our detriment.

Mark recorded a similar conversation between Jesus and His twelve apostles (Mark 9:33-37) about the value of respecting little children. But in that conversation, the Twelve complained that they had witnessed another adult speaking and working in Jesus' name, and they had told him to stop because he wasn't one of them (Mark 9:38). They were probably correct in their concern that the other man's faith wasn't as fully developed as their own. However, Jesus told them *not* to stop such people from speaking out. And He added, "If anyone causes one of these little ones— those who believe in me—to stumble, it would be better for them if a large millstone were hung around their neck and they were thrown into the sea" (Mark 9:39-42).

It's evident that Jesus had intense, compassionate concern for children, which isn't surprising, yet here we see equal fondness for *spiritual* children . . . of any age. If you're up in years, yet just now beginning to hear and apply the truths of Scripture in godly living, be assured that you have the full support of a loving and forgiving heavenly Father. Don't get stalled out at this level; keep advancing in your spiritual journey.

You'll discover that it's relatively easy to understand the teachings of Jesus and Scripture, but it can be considerably harder to consistently apply them. Jesus' disciples were with Him constantly. They not only witnessed all His miracles and heard His teaching, they also had private access to ask Him questions and gain additional insight after the crowds had gone home. Still, they repeatedly failed to practice what He preached. (I don't know about you, but that's very encouraging to me! I can relate to them.)

We've just seen that Jesus tried to impress on His closest followers the importance of respecting children—both little kids and those who were at a Child stage spiritually. Not long afterward, Jesus was teaching when people started bringing their children to Him, wanting Him to bless them. The disciples knew (or *thought* they knew) that Jesus had more important things to do than waste His time with kids, so they tried to act as bouncers and short-circuit any attempts to let mere children interfere with Jesus' ministry. Again, they were caught off guard by His unexpected response:

> People were bringing little children to Jesus for him to place his hands on them, but the disciples rebuked them. When Jesus saw this, he was indignant. He said to them, "Let the little children come to me, and do not hinder them, for the kingdom of God belongs to such as these. Truly I tell you, anyone who will not receive the kingdom of God like a little child will never enter it." And he took the children in his arms, placed his hands on them and blessed them. (Mark 10:13-16)

After everything Jesus had taught them about the warmth and breadth of His love, the disciples began shooing away parents and their children. This time Jesus became "indignant." He rebuked them in a flash of grief and anger. He didn't get angry very often, especially at the group He was preparing to carry on with His mission after His death, but in this case, they were missing an essential truth. The kingdom of God isn't established on the same power structure as human kingdoms. The main requirement for entrance isn't power; in fact, it's the opposite: childlike faith. A relationship with Jesus trumps status, control, power, wealth, accomplishment, or any other human standard.

The apostles should have known better, but then, so should we. How many times have you been in a group of adults discussing politics, world events, sports, or even something from the Bible, when a child wanders in wanting to show you something and get a little attention? Is he summarily dismissed, or told to wait until later? I doubt that I've ever been busier than Jesus was when He was on earth teaching and healing, but even when He was very busy, His response to children was to pick them up to love them . . . and then hold them up as examples.

The disciples' attempted dismissal of eager kids was especially egregious because the parents were only seeking a blessing from Jesus. They were attempting to get closer, but Jesus' followers were making it harder rather than easier. We can learn a lesson of what *not* to do by noting the disciples' response. But for anyone who's at a spiritual Child stage, the lesson is that Jesus cares for you immensely, and always invites you to come closer to Him. On this foundation, we're prepared for one of the most transformative lessons a Christ-follower can learn: the lesson of obedience.

A New Set of Clothes

You might be a spiritual child if you're learning the value of your own life and the initiative of sharing it in ways other people can experience. Spiritual children still need feeding, of course, but now they've learned how to feed themselves. They still need to be clothed, but now they're learning how to dress themselves. Growing in do-it-yourself initiative is something the Bible calls obedience. That's when we, by God's power, align our choices and behavior to God's plan.

Growing in do-it-yourself initiative is something the Bible calls obedience. That's when we, by God's power, align our choices and behavior to God's plan.

Paul uses that illustration when he writes about "clothing ourselves in Christ." In fact, I think he's speaking to spiritual children about taking the next step in their journey when he writes: "Clothe yourselves with the Lord Jesus, and do not think about how to gratify the desires of the flesh" (Romans 13:14). He illustrates the changed life that Christ offers by comparing it to taking off an old, filthy, stinking set of clothes, being washed clean, and putting on a fresh, new outfit. In another letter, he adds,

"You were taught, with regard to your former way of life, to put off your old self, which is being corrupted by its deceitful desires; to be made new in the attitude of your minds; and to put on the new self, created to be like God in true righteousness and holiness" (Ephesians 4:22-24). The new "clothes" represent a new way of thinking, believing, and living. (See Ephesians 4:25-32.) The point is that as a new child of God, you have a choice of how you continue to clothe yourself.

Many of the changes we need to make between spiritual Childhood and full maturity are evident. We're probably already well aware of any bitterness, rage, brawling, and slander, and we know we need to eliminate those harmful reactions. As we grow, we're more in tune with God's heart, and we're more aware of the ways we displease Him. Before, we didn't even notice, but now we're grieved and we turn more readily to God to experience the forgiveness Christ has already granted us on the cross.

Spiritual childhood offers a new level of insight. When our hearts are soft and eager to absorb the wonders of God's kingdom, we're able to learn more than just the things we can see and determine on our own. God reveals deeper and more specific applications of truth. Matthew recorded this prayer of Jesus: "I praise you Father, Lord of heaven and earth, because you have hidden these things from the wise and learned, and revealed them to little children. Yes, Father, for this is what you were pleased to do" (Matthew 11:25-26).

How can little kids know more than the "wise and learned"? It's not so much a matter of knowledge, but instead, of comprehension. Jesus taught thousands of people when He was on earth. He healed an untold number of them. He spent time with all kinds of people: lowly lepers, prostitutes, despised tax collectors, Roman centurions, educated scribes, Sadducees and Pharisees, and even the highest national leaders during His trials. But when Jesus asked His disciples who everyone thought He was, no one was sure. A reincarnation of John the Baptist? Elijah? Jeremiah? Some other prophet?

Then Jesus asked them point blank, "But what about you? Who do you say I am?"

Peter spoke for the group: "You are the Messiah, the Son of the living God."

Jesus told him, "Blessed are you, Simon son of Jonah, for this was not revealed to you by flesh and blood, but by my Father in heaven" (Matthew 16:13-17).

Crowds of people heard the same teachings the disciples heard, and they witnessed the same miracles, but only a few of them were spiritually attuned enough to receive God's revelation that Jesus was, indeed, the Messiah everyone was hoping for. When Jesus died after a three-year public ministry, the number of "believers" was only about 120 (Acts 1:15), although with the arrival and indwelling of the Holy Spirit, the church quickly began to grow. However, believers can still be "nearsighted and blind" to the things of God if they lose their childlike faith (2 Peter 1:5-9). That's why Jesus paradoxically kept telling grownups, "You need to be more like children."

Like children, we need to continue to learn, regardless of our spiritual stage. We'll see in a few more chapters that those in the Child stage aren't the only ones who grow up in family life. Parents do, too—at the same time as kids, but on different levels. Family life is an incubator for leadership development that helps everyone get better in leading their own lives.

Maybe you've seen these five steps of leadership development:

Step 1—I do, you watch. We talk.

Step 2—I do, you help. We talk.

Step 3—You do, I help. We talk.

Step 4—You do, I watch. We talk.

Step 5—You do, someone else watches. The two of you talk.

This is a pattern parents can follow to help their kids lead their own lives well. It's also a process spiritual mentors can use to help disciples grow. Or, to say it another way, it's how we can help children *let their little light shine, and do it themselves.*

The Basics

As usual, the parallels between biological and spiritual life are very close. Those who care for children and observe the necessary elements for their thriving may list many essentials, but the article, "What Every Child Needs for Good Mental Health," narrows down the list. To build confidence, the author recommends:

Praise Them

Encouraging children's first steps or their ability to learn a new game helps them develop a desire to explore and learn about their surroundings. Allow children to explore and play in a safe area where they cannot get hurt. Assure them by smiling and talking to them often. Be an active participant in their activities. Your attention helps build their self-confidence and self-esteem.

Set Realistic Goals

Young children need realistic goals that match their ambitions with their abilities. With your help, older children can choose activities that test their abilities and increase their self-confidence.

Be Honest

Do not hide your failures from your children. It is important for them to know that we all make mistakes. It can be very reassuring to know that adults are not perfect.

Avoid Sarcastic Remarks

If a child loses a game or fails a test, find out how he or she feels about the situation. Children may get discouraged and need a pep talk. Later, when they are ready, talk and offer assurance.

Be an Encourager

Help children not only strive to do their best, but also to enjoy the process. Trying new activities teaches children about teamwork, self-esteem, and new skills.[13]

If you're at this stage spiritually, are you in this kind of environment? If you care for someone at this stage, are you providing this kind of input?

A Few Words of Caution

We've seen that children are enthusiastic learners and are often determined to do things for themselves. Spiritual childhood is a period of attempting to absorb and apply more of God's truth to everyday life; however, this eagerness can sometimes lead to premature or even erroneous conclusions.

For example, let's reconsider Jesus' challenge in Matthew 5:16: "Let your light shine before others, that they may see your good deeds and glorify your Father in heaven" (Matthew 5:14-16). To spiritually young ears, that may sound like we earn God's approval by doing good things, but nothing can be further from the truth.

One core lesson of being a child of God is that we become God's children by grace through faith, not works. We don't earn forgiveness or salvation from God by keeping the rules or by doing what's right. Good deeds don't earn God's favor. What's our motivation for obedience, then? It's this: we do what's right because God's light is already shining from the inside out, and we obey out of gratitude for God's love, not to earn God's love. Believers at the spiritual Child stage need to be taught this distinction, and mature believers need to point them to the grand truths of Scripture and assure them:

➤ "It is by grace you have been saved, through faith—and this is not from yourselves, it is the gift of God—not by works, so that no one can boast" (Ephesians 2:8-9).

➤ "When the kindness and love of God our Savior appeared, he saved us, not because of righteous things we had done, but because of his mercy. He saved us through the washing of rebirth and renewal by the Holy Spirit, whom he poured out on us generously through Jesus Christ our Savior" (Titus 3:4-6).

➤ "[God] has saved us and called us to a holy life—not because of anything we have done but because of his own purpose and grace" (2 Timothy 1:9).

Of course, inquisitive children want to ask follow-up questions. In this case, they'll wonder why, if those works aren't impressing God, so much emphasis is placed on good works in parts of the Bible. That's the time to follow up the Ephesians 2:8-9 passage with verse 10: "For we are God's handiwork, created in Christ Jesus to do good works, which God prepared in advance for us to do."

Good works are part of the salvation train, but they're the cars and caboose, not the engine!

Good works are part of the salvation train, but they're the cars and caboose, not the engine! That's what we learn in spiritual childhood. Even spiritual children can understand that if God doled out salvation and other blessings based only on how much we do for Him, Christian life would become one long, ongoing competition to impress Him. In that case, we would never become the "one body" He desires as we jostle to become holier than the people around us and lobby to be God's "teacher's pet." How much better it is to do good works because we have a good and gracious Father whose life is now growing in us! Remember: obedience is aligning my choices and behavior to God's plan by God's power.

Another passage that tends to confuse younger believers is Philippians 2:12-13: "My dear friends, as you have always obeyed . . . continue to work out your salvation with fear and trembling, for it is God who works in you to will and to act in order to fulfill his good purpose." Does that sound scary to you? It can sound threatening to spiritual children when they begin to hear things like "work" . . . "obey" . . . "fear and trembling."

But wait! Let's again make sure we get the whole context so we can clarify this for less mature Bible readers. Don't just read the first half and stop. Finish the thought: *God is at work in you,* and *He shows up to inspire and empower you to obey Him.* This passage doesn't say you're working *for* your salvation. There's a big difference between *working out* your salvation and *working for* it.

Believers already have salvation by God's power and grace. To work it out means it's already in—it's already in you. So now God is working in you, changing you, growing you according to His good purpose, and you're working it out. Just think about that for a moment. Can you imagine our almighty, infinite God working in you? As we try to comprehend such an incredible thought, that's where the healthy fear of God comes from. It's enough to make even the most mature believer tremble. But what does that mean?

It's not unusual for power sources to have signs in bold, black, block letters that warn, HIGH VOLTAGE. When we get near something so powerful, we need to be aware and pay attention. There's absolutely nothing wrong with the source of power, but it's so awesome that we need to notice. That's what Paul's doing here. He's saying, "Caution! Let's never lose respect for God's awesome power in and through our lives." As God works in us, we then work it out by living obediently to Him and His purpose. Good deeds are the natural result of a confident relationship with God . . . but never the origin.

I like the way Corrie ten Boom defines responsibility: "It is not my ability, but my response to God's ability that counts." That's what we learn in being obedient as God's children.

In Summary

During spiritual childhood, Jesus helps you learn to hear His voice. He once told some of His critics who were resisting His teaching, "My sheep listen to my voice; I know them, and they follow me" (John 10:27). That's obedience. For those who want to hear and follow Jesus, God's Spirit helps us make that connection. Maybe you've heard people talk about "the promptings of God," or "that still, small voice." Well, during spiritual childhood you begin to learn how to recognize the voice of God.

Perhaps you've heard of a horse whisperer—someone with a special gift of communicating with the animal to make it more responsive and calm it during frightening experiences. Well, God is a Child whisperer . . . a *spiritual* child whisperer. His Spirit (the living Word) speaks through the Bible (His written Word) to mold us and make us more like Jesus (the incarnate Word). In other words, Jesus, through His Spirit and His Scripture, calls spiritual children to be obedient.

The way to a happy spiritual childhood is to learn obedience. An old hymn reminds us to "trust and obey, for there's no other way to be happy in Jesus but to trust and obey." But Christian obedience doesn't involve God cracking the whip and forcing you to do something you don't want to do. No, no, no. When you begin to see how your life is being transformed by the Spirit of God working in you, you're glad to comply with whatever He asks.

Think of it like this: Your faith is like a car key, and God is like the car's engine. Obedience is the turn of the key that fires the ignition and puts your car in motion while God is at work under the hood in your everyday life. Obedience releases God's power that's already at work within you. And what is God's power working to do? Remember Paul's comment to the Philippians: "It is God who works in you to will and to act in order to fulfill his good purpose" (Philippians 2:12-13).

In other words, God first works in you to create the desire to obey. If you're like me and almost everybody else I know, you'll find yourself resisting God's leadership at some points in your life. So, what can you do when you're unwilling? Here's a great prayer I've learned to pray: "Lord, I'm not really willing, but I'm willing to become willing." What an honest and powerful prayer! The Holy Spirit creates the desire to become more willing to seek God's purpose and God's presence. This is you, as a spiritual astronaut, telling Mission Control you're open and receptive to the course corrections communicated to you.

God works in us first "to will"—to help us *want* to do as He instructs— and then "to act." That means to empower your obedience, to fire the ignition that then moves the engine according to His good purpose.

My Experience

I recall several specific steps of obedience that God led me to take during my early spiritual childhood. I won't say much about each step, but I want to show you that for me it was a period of significant change, commitment, and personal growth.

A commitment to Scripture

Jesus promised that if we seek first the kingdom of God, then everything else we need will be added (Matthew 6:33). We seek God's kingdom by learning His Word to discover His will, and I sensed God telling me, "Start every day with Me, Bill. Start every day in My Word." As a spiritual child, I learned how to feed myself in Scripture. Just like I know my kitchen and where to look for food when I'm hungry, I learned where to go in the Bible to find nourishment for my soul. The more I read Scripture, the clearer I heard God's direction in the following steps.

Baptism

One of my first steps of faith was being baptized as a declaration: "Christ is now alive in me and I'm following Him." In my spiritual journey, I had been a newborn, then an infant, and then a toddler, but at the spiritual Child stage, I took the step of obedience to follow Jesus in water baptism.

Tithing

Next I sensed God telling me, "Trust Me with your tithe. The first dime of every dollar, Bill, give it to Me. Why? Because where your treasure is, that's where your heart will be. Your heart will be more fully with Me when you trust Me with your treasures. Give and it will be given to you, a good measure, pressed down, shaken together, and running over." (See Matthew 6:21 and Luke 6:38.)

Seeking forgiveness

I knew God wanted me to ask forgiveness and make amends for hurts I had caused. I went to people I'd sinned against, apologized, and asked them how I could make it right. It was humbling, but it was necessary. These actions cleared up hurt, anger, and fear, so the relationships could grow—and I found God to be faithful as I obeyed Him in this way. (See Luke 19:1-10 to see the story the Lord used to lead me in this healing work.)

Watching my words

The Bible says, "Let your conversation be always full of grace, seasoned with salt, so that you may know how to answer everyone" (Colossians 4:6). At the time, I was using some salty language . . . but not in the biblical sense! At God's direction, I stopped using profanity and started using more grace-filled words to express myself (Ephesians 4:29).

Respecting my body.

It's an awesome discovery to learn that our bodies are temples of the Holy Spirit and that we now belong to God (1 Corinthians 6:19-20). God showed me that spiritual growth requires physical commitments as well. He said to honor Him with my body: don't get drunk, don't abuse drugs, and treat women with respect rather than lust. Instead, I was to be filled with the Holy Spirit (Ephesians 5:18).

Telling others

As I began to see positive changes in my life, God said, "I want you to share your story, to talk about My good news with others so they can know Me, too."

In all these areas, do you know what He was doing? He was teaching me obedience . . . how to listen and follow . . . how to turn the key of faith through the action of obedience so I could access His power to keep growing to become more like Him. Remember: obedience is aligning my choices and behavior with God's plan by God's power.

What's Your Experience?

Jesus promised His followers: "Whoever has my commands and keeps them is the one who loves me. The one who loves me will be loved by my Father, and I too will love them and show myself to them" (John 14:21). That's a lot of love crammed into a few words, right? And Jesus is speaking of the highest level of love: *agape* love, which is God's quality of love. Do you want more of the *agape* love of God in your experience? Jesus says it's right here in the act of obedience. And as an added bonus, He promises to show himself to those who obey Him. That's a pretty sweet promise!

Obedience is God's way of growing us up in His love and showing us more of who He is. It enlarges our capacity to know Him better. I've learned this personally, but I can assure you I'm nobody special. God didn't treat me this way because I'm rare and unique. This is how He wants every one of his children to grow.

One further word of insight I learned from my spiritual childhood: Don't confuse the filling of the Holy Spirit with a feeling. Feelings may indeed accompany being filled by God's Spirit in living an obedient life, but if you don't feel bubbly or spiritual, it doesn't mean God isn't filling you with His Spirit's power and presence. Trust that obeys, regardless of how you feel, is how to be happy in Jesus.

How about you? Have you learned how to feed yourself and how to listen for God's voice? Does the Spirit (the living Word) speak to you through the Bible (the written Word) to make you more like Jesus (the incarnate Word)? And if so, do you respond in obedience?

Information without application brings stagnation, which is why some people get stuck in their spiritual childhood. They gain knowledge, but they're disobedient. They don't respond when Jesus invites them to act in faith—and a disobedient child who gets stuck isn't a happy child.

However, information *with* application brings transformation. That's spiritual growth. So, the primary lesson to learn in your spiritual childhood is simply *obedience*. If you want to continue growing and making progress in your spiritual journey, obedience is the only way.

Let your little light shine by taking the initiative so others can see your good deeds and experience God as their good, good father, too. Hide it under a bushel? No! You've got to let it shine!

STAGE	LESSON
Godparent	
Grandparent	
Parent	
Adult	
Adolescent	
Preteen	
Child	Put knowledge into action. Obey God in active faith.
Toddler	Learn to walk in faith and talk to God in prayer as you grow in community with God and others.
Infant	Receive nourishing care from your loving heavenly Father and other spiritual "parents" who want to help you grow.
Newborn	Be born again and receive God's wonderful new life.

ADVENTURE PAGES

Pilot's Flight Plan

1. What are some of your favorite songs from your childhood, Christian or not? How have they influenced your life?

2. When you read about Jesus' interactions with little children, how does it compare to how you were treated as a child? Explain your answer.

3. Since becoming a believer, to what extent do you feel you have "clothed yourself in Christ"? What have you already done to clothe yourself, and what do you still need to do?

4. If a young person asked you to explain the connection between salvation and good works, how would you explain it?

    How would you explain the instruction to "work out your salvation in fear and trembling"?

5. Have you ever been stuck and unable to continue growing spiritually because you weren't obedient to something God had instructed you to do? What was the problem?

    Do you feel stuck right now? If so, what do you need to do to continue your spiritual transformation?

Course Correction

If you only do one thing, do this: As you read this chapter, the Holy Spirit probably brought at least one thing to mind in which He wants you to obey. If there are more than one, choose one, determine how you'll obey, and then do it. Don't wait. Do it!

Captain's Log

If you're helping a spiritual child grow, I suggest:

➤ In this stage, people are often very eager to please God. Help the person clarify how God is leading him or her to obey.

➤ Provide "easy on-ramps" of ways the person can pray, give, and serve.

➤ Be sure to communicate that disobedience is significant, but God loves, forgives, restores, and redirects.

YOU MAY BE A PRETEEN IF . . .

PRETEEN

"To find the will of God is the greatest discovery.
To do the will of God is the greatest achievement."

—George Washington Truett

Walter Abercrombie was a star running back for the Bears at Baylor University in Waco, Texas. When he graduated, he was the #1 draft pick of the Pittsburgh Steelers, where he played professional football for years. A Baylor alum and friend sent me an article Abercrombie wrote titled "It Is Good!" Here's the story he told:

A powerful African king had a close friend with whom he had grown up who was known for always having the most positive attitude. No matter the situation, good or bad, the friend would see the positive and then would say, "It is good, it is good." One day the two were out hunting. The friend loaded the guns and then handed them to the king to fire. One of the guns malfunctioned when the king pulled the trigger and it blew off his thumb. The friend, in characteristic fashion, remarked, "Oh my king, it is good!" But the king became irate and shouted, "No! It is *not* good!" In a rage, the king had his friend arrested and thrown into the dungeon.

A year later the king was touring an unsettled wilderness region in Africa where he was taken captive by a tribe of cannibals. They tied him up, bound him to a stake, and surrounded him with wood, preparing to make a meal of him. But before they set fire to the wood, one of them noticed that his thumb was missing. They were a superstitious tribe and never ate anyone that was not whole. Because of the missing thumb, the cannibal chief let him go.

Upon his return home, the king immediately went to the dungeon where his friend was still being held. He had him released and said, "Oh, you were right. It was good that my thumb was blown off." He told his friend about his ordeal with the cannibals and how he regretted sending him to prison. Then the king said, "It was bad for me to do this to you, my friend." But his friend disagreed: "No, my king, it is good!"

The confused king protested, "What do you mean? What could possibly be good about spending a year in a dungeon?"

His friend replied, "If you had not sent me to prison, I would have been with you . . . and they would have eaten me because I have all my fingers. So you see, my king, it is good!"[14]

Good story, huh? Walter said the first time he told the story had been years ago while he talked with someone about how important it is to hold on to your faith in the midst of troubles. And these are troubling times, aren't they? Faith gets us through some difficult situations and distressing circumstances. Even when the outlook isn't so good, we should never stop believing that in all things God works for the good of those who love Him (Romans 8:28).

I wanted you to hear this story, but even more, I wanted to tell you *why* Walter wrote about it. In the article, he said he hadn't told the story for so long that he had forgotten it. But one day his twenty-three-year-old son reminded him of it. Walter had told it when his son was in his tween-age years—during that transitional period of early adolescence somewhere between eight and fourteen years of age. The story's significance had lodged in the boy's mind all that time to become meaningful years later when he reminded his father of its truth.

A Change Is Going to Come

Anybody who's had a child that age knows that preteens can't be parented in the same way they were when they were younger. They've reached a new level in their development, with different potentials to be considered and different needs to be addressed: identity needs (Who am I?), community needs (Where do I belong? Where do I fit in?), and purpose and meaning needs (Why am I here? What's my destiny?). A new level of cognitive ability develops as their minds become increasingly open, responsive, and able to understand more than just straightforward, simple truths. They would be drawn to a story like Walter Abercrombie's that poses reasons why it might not always be such a tragedy to lose a thumb or to spend time in jail for seemingly no good reason. It's probably why the story stuck in Abercrombie's son's memory.

Who am I?
Where do I belong?
Where do I fit in?
Why am I here?
What's my destiny?

And then, at that age, kids contend with puberty. Talk about identity issues! The big question becomes, "What's going on with my body?" A whole new physical transformation is unfolding. (So is an emotional one, but the physical changes usually demand full attention at first.)

Girls usually begin puberty before boys, around age nine or ten and lasting four or five years. Breast development is usually the first sign. The hips get wider and the body becomes curvier. Menstruation is usually one of the final changes.

Boys are slower to begin puberty, typically at around age twelve, with initial signs being the growth of the testicles and scrotum. Boys, too, undergo about four years of physical transformation as their muscles grow, facial hair begins to sprout, and their voices deepen.

Both boys and girls can expect a growth spurt—two to three inches a year for a few years, and rapid growth can make them awkward and clumsy. Many get acne for a time. Hair begins to grow in new places. They begin to sweat more, and body odor may become an issue (for some, a big issue!).

The good news is that after any misery that puberty may cause for the individuals (and their parents), they are essentially physiological adults when it's over. They won't get much taller, and they're capable of sexual reproduction (which creates a whole new level of concern for parents).

As challenging as such extreme physical changes are to begin with, the hormonal shifts also initiate a lot of emotional changes for most preteens and their families. One of the biggest frustrations for a child going through puberty is that the rate of change—both physical and emotional—varies widely from person to person. Children naturally compare themselves to others. Those who develop first may feel terribly self-conscious, but so will those who are late bloomers.

Navigating the Preteen Years

Parents need to be especially patient and understanding about "moodiness" and other emotional challenges during this period. Here are a few suggestions for helping a child through this stage of early adolescence.

Expect emotional turbulence.

The preteen and early teen years can be volatile, full of emotional drama. Feelings can be intense and unpredictable. Puberty initiates mood swings (sometimes extreme) and strong feelings, including an onset of sexual thoughts and urges. Your child can be exhilarated at one moment but deeply discouraged the next.

Adapt your discipline.

Discipline becomes more challenging. Until now, a parent could settle most concerns or disputes with the child simply by saying, "Because I'm the mama [or daddy]," or, "Because I said so, that's why." But parents find out pretty quickly that particular response doesn't work anymore. This is the stage when "the wonder years" transition into the "I wonder what happened" years.

Initiate the delicate conversations.

It's difficult enough for a child to cope with the physical changes taking place, much less mentioning them to Mom and Dad. Observant parents gently bring up sensitive issues before the child goes looking for information elsewhere. Start with some of the practical basics: "I can't believe how quickly you're growing. Would you like me to show you how to shave?" "Whenever you're ready, let's have a mother/daughter day to have lunch together and go pick out a bra." Deal with hygiene issues and other matters as they arise. If your kids learn that you're open to talking about such things, they're more likely to value your advice as weightier issues arise . . . like sex. (More on that conversation in the next chapter.)

Stay close even as you're letting go.

It can be frustrating to devote a dozen or so years to raising a good son or daughter, only to see child at this age bond with new friends and appear to have no further use for their parents. Friends suddenly seem to become more important than breathing or eating. It's nothing personal; the child is trying to establish his or her own identity, which includes trying new things and testing boundaries. Counselors say that expected behaviors for preteens can include fights with siblings (as they sort out their differences of opinion and identify their property), increased peer influence (be-cause they want to feel accepted and valued), and risk-taking (whether attempting new tricks at the skateboard park or dabbling in "forbidden" behaviors like smoking, drinking, and drug use). The challenge is to give them adequate room to grow while ensuring they don't get involved with the wrong friends or anything they shouldn't be doing. (It's a high-wire act for most parents.)

Remember that online influence may be stronger than you realize.

With the preponderance of smartphones, it's difficult for parents to monitor Internet usage. Even if your child doesn't have one, his or her friends surely do. Not only do preteens have round-the-clock access to information (or misinformation) about vaping, drugs, alcohol, sexual behavior, and other temptations, but many are subject to cyber-bullying, online threats, and public humiliation. On one hand, parents shouldn't overreact to a preteen's mood swings, but they must also remain alert to signs of serious trouble in their children's lives.

The Perils of Spiritual Preteens

It can be painful to remember what it was like to be a biological pre-teen, although it's helpful to dredge up those memories when it's time to comfort a child going through the same traumas—and being a spiritual preteen is not much easier.

In fact, I think the entire book of 1 Corinthians was written to a church full of spiritual preteens. This church wasn't *growing* in Christ, they were *regressing*. Paul begins by pointing out their underlying attitude of jealou-sy and worldliness, and as he continues, he spells out a lot of additional specific problems. It seems to me that the whole letter addresses spiritual adolescence. Paul hardly finishes his greeting in this long letter before he begins jumping into their issues. He has received word that the Corinthian church members were picking sides and quarreling over which Christian leader was most worthy of their support, and he immediately sets out to convince them to resolve their differences:

> I appeal to you, brothers and sisters, in the name of our Lord Jesus Christ, that all of you agree with one another in what you say and that there be no divisions among you, but that you be perfectly united in mind and thought. . . . What I mean is this: One of you says, "I follow Paul"; another, "I follow Apollos"; another, "I follow Cephas"; still another, "I follow Christ." (1 Corinthians 1:10, 12)

That means at least four groups were competing, comparing, and picking fights in the church. Perhaps there were more. As a pastor, I get it. They each had their reasons to believe they were right. Paul had founded their church, so he naturally had a following. Apollos was a powerful preacher, probably exciting to listen to. But then, Cephas (another name for Simon Peter) had spent three years with Jesus, and none of the others could say that. And of course, there was the super-spiritual subgroup (a staple in many churches). They claimed to "follow Christ"—surely superior to all the rest. But despite any loyalties and good intentions these groups had, they were wrong to allow their personal preferences to destroy the unity of the church.

Paul wasn't finished with them. Not long after his opening critique, he let them know that the longer they failed to come to any agreement on their leadership issues, the more their spiritual progress would suffer:

> Brothers and sisters, I could not address you as people who live by the Spirit but as people who are still worldly—mere infants in Christ. I gave you milk, not solid food, for you were not yet ready for it. Indeed, you are still not ready. You are still worldly. For since there is jealousy and quarreling among you, are you not worldly? Are you not acting like mere humans? (1 Corinthians 3:1-3)

Here's a church filled with people who have known the Lord for some time. They've been following Jesus long enough that they should be feeding themselves. They've grown to the point where they should be eating solids and building kingdom muscle. But instead, they're fighting with their sibling brothers and sisters in Christ.

You're acting like it's someone else's job to give you what you want.

Using this church in Corinth as an example, I think *spiritual* preteen behavior becomes evident: you should be responsibly feeding yourself from God's Word and practicing spiritual disciplines, but you're acting like it's someone else's job to give you what you want. Or maybe you tend to rate and rank Christian teachers until you find a favorite, and then you feel like you don't have to pay attention to the others. This mentality is competitive and divisive. Or instead of taking responsibility for your own spiritual growth, perhaps you're stagnant and looking for someone else to blame. Any of these problems might arise during the Preteen stage, and they need to be addressed, avoided, and overcome so spiritual progress can continue.

The Potential of Spiritual Preteens

This stage also provides opportunities for tremendous growth and learning. The Bible contains very little information about the life of Jesus between His birth stories and the beginning of His public ministry at around age thirty, but one story offers insight into Jesus as a preteen. Jesus at twelve years old is dealing with the questions all young people struggle to answer: Who am I? Where do I belong? What am I here to do? Here is Luke's account:

Every year Jesus' parents went to Jerusalem for the Festival of the Passover. When he was twelve years old, they went up to the festival, according to the custom. After the festival was over, while his parents were returning home, the boy Jesus stayed behind in Jerusalem, but they were unaware of it. Thinking he was in their company, they traveled on for a day. Then they began looking for him among their relatives and friends. When they did not find him, they went back to Jerusalem to look for him. After three days they found him in the temple courts, sitting among the teachers, listening to them and asking them questions. Everyone who heard him was amazed at his understanding and his answers. When his parents saw him, they were astonished. His mother said to him, "Son, why have you treated us like this? Your father and I have been anxiously searching for you."

"Why were you searching for me?" he asked. "Didn't you know I had to be in my Father's house?" But they did not understand what he was saying to them.

Then he went down to Nazareth with them and was obedient to them. But his mother treasured all these things in her heart. And Jesus grew in wisdom and stature, and in favor with God and man. (Luke 2:41-52)

The story introduces us to Jesus at puberty, entering early adolescence. I hope you hear the humor and feel the humanity in this part of the story. Dr. Luke wants us to hear it and feel it as his Gospel shows us Jesus growing in identity, community, and purpose and meaning. This is a rite of passage story in three parts: celebration, separation, and consecration. In fact, three stories are evolving simultaneously. Jesus' personal rite of passage is placed directly parallel to the nation of Israel and to His family through his mother, Mary.

This account takes place at Passover, the defining moment in Israel's *identity* when God miraculously freed His people from slavery in Egypt, marking them as God's *community* and then calling them to their *destiny*, through whom God would reveal himself to the world. The Passover *celebration* noted their *separation* from Egypt, effected by the blood of the lamb that was placed on their doorposts. The Feast of Unleavened Bread that immediately followed Passover reminded them that they were to walk in *consecration* to God. They were supposed to walk with God into their future without delay. Don't waste time. Eat unleavened bread so you don't have to wait for the dough to rise. In other words, "Come with Me *now!*"

Jesus' story is parallel to Israel's. This Passover celebration is where we see Jesus' first clear awareness of His *identity* as God's Son. At Jesus' Preteen stage, we see Him moving from simply *receiving* the care of His village and His parents to a new level of *choosing* his own *community* and then finding His own voice in it. It's a *celebration* of a coming of age, but it's also a *separation* from His biological parents. Mary, especially, feels the separation anxiety. She wants to know, "Why have you treated us like this?" Jesus responds with a question of His own: "Why were you searching for me? Why didn't you know where I would be?" (If you've parented a preteen, this classic exchange of "why?" questions between parent and child undoubtedly sounds very familiar.)

As Luke records this story, he uses three words that are full of emotion:

➤ *Amazed* means stupefied or dumbfounded.

➤ *Astonished* means panicked, almost frantic.

➤ *Anxious* means tormented with distress.

Do those emotions sound like puberty or early adolescence to you? Maybe so, but in this case, it was the adults in the story who were having these responses! That leads us to Mary's story.

The *celebration* of Jesus' rite of passage was also a *separation*. Mary's little boy was no longer a boy. Luke says that she "treasured all these things in her heart." To "treasure" something is to set it apart, which is also a definition of the word *consecration*. Mary was stepping up into a new level of *consecration* before God. She begins to realize that her *destiny* no longer lies in raising the boy, but in releasing the man. She intuitively asked the question almost all parents ask: "How do I hold on while letting go?"

Jesus' destiny, riding parallel with Mary's, is found in *consecration* as well. The Spirit within Jesus was compelling Him, defining His destiny. Jesus' question, "Didn't you know I had to be in my Father's house?" is much more forceful in the original language. Literally, it reads, "I *must* be in my Father's things." This will not be the only time He speaks with such determination, using the powerful word "must." Later He will say:

> ➤ "I must proclaim the good news of the kingdom of God" (Luke 4:43);

> ➤ "Zacchaeus, . . . I must stay at your house today" (Luke 19:5);

> ➤ "The Son of Man must suffer many things . . . and he must be killed and on the third day be raised to life" (Luke 9:22).

Luke concluded his account of Jesus' preteen years by saying that Jesus grew in wisdom, stature, favor with God, and favor with others. That moves Jesus into the phase of adolescence, which we'll discuss in the next chapter, but the expectation for those still in the early adolescent, Preteen stage is well summed up in Proverbs 9:6: "Leave your simple ways and you will live; walk in the way of insight." Spiritual preteens are taking steps of greater obedience and getting clarity of focus on their life's mission from God.

Lessons from Early Adolescence

Are you in your period of spiritual preteen growth? If so, how do you know? Well, you'd be asking questions like "Who am I, really?" and then finding your identity in Christ. You'll be wondering, "Where do I belong?" and then finding a Christian community that supports and promotes your spiritual growth. You're asking, "What am I here to do?" and you're realizing the need to fulfill your destiny and accomplish your mission in the will of God.

As a spiritual preteen, you're not quite an adolescent, but you're very close. To keep moving forward, you have to take responsibility for doing the will of God with your life. You choose for yourself . . . finding your *own* voice in doing it.

If you think you may be experiencing your spiritual preteen life right now, you're probably wondering, *How do I step out of my spiritual childhood? How do I rise to the next level?* Easy answer: as you've been doing so far, continue following Christ and His voice. The big question for us at this level is, "Are you listening and obeying, stepping out in faith as you've been taught?"

Obedience was the lesson of childhood, remember? First you learn how to listen to God's voice and obey it. Then the question becomes, "Are you connecting in *mentoring* relationships where you continue interacting with the truths of God?" At this stage, you're no longer just receiving teaching, but you're sharing what *you* think with those who care for your spiritual growth. You're asking lots of questions. You're discovering and clarifying God's answers, and then you're expressing in your own voice what you believe God wants you to do, just as Jesus did with His parents at the Jerusalem temple. Ken Dodson, whom I mentioned earlier, was a spiritual parent to me in this stage of my growth and I also had other mentors, as will you.

You may occasionally find yourself in a new level of conflict with your spiritual parents, much like what occurs between biological parents and children during the preteen years. Maybe you don't even know exactly why, but because you're finding and now defining your own relationship with God, you're starting to ask, "Why? Why do we believe that? Why does it matter?" As you begin to own the answers for yourself, you may discover that you don't necessarily agree with everything you've been taught. That's okay. You're finding your own voice and stepping up into your destiny as it becomes clearer what truly following Christ means for *your* life.

Concerns for Spiritual Parents

When children go through early adolescence, or when someone is at this level spiritually, the parent(s) may not think they're making much of an impact. That's why I opened this chapter with the story Walter Abercrombie told his preteen years ago. Walter had completely forgotten that he'd ever told that story to his son—but his son didn't forget. The story is also a reminder that even though preteens sometimes question whether their parents are really concerned about their best interests, these kids need to believe that, just maybe, their parents have the wisdom to see a bigger picture when they assure them, "It is good. Things will be okay." During early adolescence—biological and spiritual— some of the stories that were told and embedded in your childhood are now being recalled, tested, and proven.

> When you're a child, you believe the Bible stories because that's what you're taught, but at this stage, you want more details and explanations.

The Preteen stage is an awkward transition between childhood and spiritual adulthood. When you're a child, you believe the Bible stories because that's what you're taught, but at this stage, you want more details and explanations. You ask, "What does this mean?" "How did that happen?" "Why do we believe that?"

Don't be alarmed if that's how you're feeling. It may feel like a crisis of faith, but it's not. It's a normal part of growth. It's a growing pain. Your spiritual cognitive capacities must continue to grow so you can learn how to love God with all your mind. But expect to undergo a bit of confusion, and even some doubt, as you begin to own your faith for yourself. Also, remember that your spiritual parents are growing, too, so don't disrespect them in the process.

Remember that at this stage, physically, kids can't help but compare their rate of growth to everyone else they know at their age. They need to realize that it's not the same for any two people. This point is also essential to remember on a spiritual level. Ask God frequently to show you how to make room for everyone to grow and become more mature-ish—whether they seem to be way ahead of you or lagging far behind. The important thing is for everyone to keep growing. That's God's desire for us.

Halfway There?

Remember this: every stage of your spiritual development builds on the previous one. Whatever lessons you learn, you'll build on in the next stage. The obedience you learn in your spiritual childhood becomes the muscle required to fulfill God's mission in the future. If you feel stalled or stagnant in your growth, I suggest you review the lessons that you've learned so far and then apply them—not just keep them in your head, but put them into action.

In fact, now that we're halfway through the mature-ish process at this stage, let's update the growth chart, review the stages so far, and see what we've learned.

STAGE	LESSON
Godparent	
Grandparent	
Parent	
Adult	
Adolescent	
Preteen	Discover who you are: your identity in Christ, where you belong, and your destiny in fulfilling God's will.
Child	Put knowledge into action. Obey God in active faith.
Toddler	Learn to walk in faith and talk to God in prayer as you grow in community with God and others.
Infant	Receive nourishing care from your loving heavenly Father and other spiritual "parents" who want to help you grow.
Newborn	Be born again and receive God's wonderful new life.

If you've met all the prerequisites, you're now equipped to move ahead to the Adolescent stage. You'll be starting the second half of the process with perhaps your biggest challenge yet.

ADVENTURE PAGES

Pilot's Flight Plan

1. Can you recall a story or lesson you learned as a preteen that has been lodged in your mind all these years? Why do you think you've remembered it?

2. Have you ever shown favoritism to one Christian pastor or leader to the exclusion of all others? How can this problem be avoided or minimized?

3. What has God shown you so far in regard to your:

    ➤ Identity?

    ➤ Community?

    ➤ Purpose and Meaning (Destiny)?

4. In what ways, if any, does your spiritual Preteen stage compare with the account of Jesus at age twelve (Luke 2:41-51)?

5. How well do you think you've completed your first five spiritual stages at this point? Are you ready to move on? If not, which stage do you feel needs additional attention?

Course Correction

If you only do one thing, do this: Find someone who isn't surprised when you ask hard questions . . . and ask them!

Captain's Log

If you're helping a spiritual preteen grow, I suggest:

➤ Welcome questions—all questions. Answer them with patience and thoroughness. If you don't know the answer, say, "I don't know, but let's find out together."

➤ At this stage, people can be very critical of some leaders and blind to the humanity of others. Help them see more objectively.

➤ Don't be the only source of wisdom and love for the spiritual preteen. Introduce him or her to other mature, loving people who can have a positive influence.

STEPPING INTO YOUR WARRIOR

ADOLESCENT

"...willing to march into hell for a heavenly cause."

—The Impossible Dream

When I was first thinking through the material in this chapter, I was preparing a message for my congregation. The very morning I was preparing my talk, I received an unexpected text message from a friend in my church who is a medical doctor:

Bill, I've been led to pray for you this morning. I just wanted to tell you that I love you, and I appreciate you very much. I'm praying for your wisdom and discernment as you lead us through these uncharted waters.

I responded:

Thank you so much. I need and appreciate your prayers and encouragement because today I'm working on a message that's about adolescence, biological and spiritual.

And to that, the good doctor sent me a two-word response: *A minefield!*

What an appropriate description of adolescence: *a minefield*. It's a word loaded with warning. A minefield is where stuff blows up . . . and you don't always see it coming or know why, when, where, or how it's going to explode. You're cautious and unsure about where to step because when you do, something unintended may happen. And if you find yourself in a minefield and manage to make your way out without any serious damage, you're forever grateful.

Doesn't that sound a lot like adolescence? Perhaps you've accompanied a child or two through this stage of life, or maybe you still have occasional nightmares about your own adolescent years. I certainly remember mine, and now that I have children of my own, I am so much more appreciative of my parents who were on the receiving end during that stage of my life.

Physical Adolescence

Adolescence has been called *the time with something to offend everyone.* It's commonly associated with teen years, although it may begin earlier and end later. It's a period of transition between child and adult, when hormones are in full swing, preparing brain and body for the challenges of adulthood.

An opinion survey was taken at the turn of the century to ask how people felt about America's teenagers. Seventy-one percent of those polled admitted that *negative* terms were the first that came to mind. However, eighty-nine percent of those responding still felt like the teenagers would eventually turn out okay.[15] Studies like this seem to confirm that although adolescence can be a difficult and traumatic period, it doesn't have the final say in how a young man or woman turns out.

Do you know what professionals say adolescents need the most? I'll give you a clue: it's perhaps the one thing adults have in least supply for them. Surveys of teenagers repeatedly show that what they need and want from adults is . . . *time.* They want their parents and other caring adults to be involved in their nurturing, learning, guidance, protection, and in directing their courage and creativity into healthy adulthood.

A report by the U.S. Council of Economic Advisers confirmed that adolescents whose parents are more involved in their lives have significantly lower rates of "problem behaviors" like smoking, alcohol and drug abuse, lying to parents, fighting, initiating sexual activity, and suicidal thoughts and actions. Although it takes time to establish emotional bonds of trust, young people need and want adults who will listen to them, who will understand them, who will value their perspectives and then coach and motivate them toward healthy self-care. Time is an investment that has a powerful and lasting payoff, yet too many parents fail to spend enough time with their adolescent children.

With all the variables in a teenager's life during adolescence, a lot can go wrong. Sometimes a parent isn't involved enough, and the child seeks attention in other places and behaviors. Other times the parent seemingly does everything possible to encourage the teenager, yet the child decides to do whatever he or she wants to do. A pastor at one of our church's other campuses has a telling, but encouraging story to tell about his biological adolescence. Rafael Then-Gea (Pastor Ralph) is the Campus Pastor of our Christ Journey congregation in Kendall. He's a trophy of God's grace, and I'm happy to share his story with you. Here's some of his adolescent journey in his own words:

As a young boy I struggled with the belief that I wasn't good enough. I would try to do good things, but I constantly fell short—and I still feel that way at times. Back then my father wasn't around much, and when he was around, he was abusive.

Yet God provided me with a mentor, a teacher, a person that walked with me. His name was Caleb, and he invited me to his church when I was ten. I accepted that invitation and I started attending regularly. When I was twelve, I made the decision to accept Christ into my life, and I was baptized. I know lots of people have stories that start out this way, and they turn out fine. But my story took a different turn.

By the time I was fourteen, I made decisions to turn away from God and from the calling that He had given me. I started hanging out with people that I shouldn't have been hanging out with. I started experimenting with different narcotics and I got into a lot of trouble. When I was fifteen I attended my last church camp (because I almost got kicked out), and I started living in this thing called shame.

My shame started pushing me further and further away from what God was calling me to do . . . further away from the people that loved me, that He had placed by my side. I started following other father figures from my former world that I thought would lead me in the right way. But I was constantly trying to earn love; I was always fighting for things that I shouldn't have been fighting for.

Yet even after I took off and I thought I was on my own road, Caleb was still there. He would pray for me, he would contact me, and he never gave up on me—even after I left the church at fifteen and decided to go to the Dominican Republic to try to start my life over on my own. While away, I was living in shame as I started falling deeper and deeper into temptation. Spiritual oppression started settling over me. I was facing many battles, and none of them were good.

But at sixteen, I came back to the United States, got my high school diploma, and then started college. I even decided to sign up for the Navy. With my diploma and college credits, I was going in as an E4 with a $10,000 signing bonus. Everything seemed great. All I had to do was complete my basics in Pensacola. However, all the plans I was making were based on my own strength.

A month before I was supposed to go, I got stabbed twice . . . at a house party . . . while I was play fighting. My life got turned upside down while I was play fighting. My wounds were severe, requiring a four-hour surgery, two pints of blood that I had to receive through transfusion, and a lengthy recovery period.

My dreams—everything I had worked so hard for—were all shattered. No more leaving for the Navy, much less a signing bonus. Within a month, I dropped from 218 pounds to 146 pounds.

But believe it or not, this story has a happy ending. When I woke up from surgery, I began to reconnect with people who loved me. Caleb showed up to see me the very next day. He never gave up on me. He was always there. A friend from my childhood named Tracy welcomed me back to church with a big hug and tears rolling down his face. One of the church's former pastors who had been a Navy Seal saw something in me I couldn't see in myself, and he pushed me to see the vision that God had for my life—a future far better than my own limited plans. God put many spiritually strong and encouraging people in my life, including Liz, a wonderful woman who would become my wife. Liz would constantly push me to be better and for us to grow closer to Christ.

My story started with shame, betrayal, and heartbreak. I literally had to fight for my own life. Thank God it didn't end there. I am thankful because during those hard moments, God surrounded me with people who were loving and never gave up on me. They patiently coached me and helped me through the turbulence so that I could arrive where God wanted me to be. I am thankful for all the leaders that walked next to me during those hard times and helped me see things I hadn't seen in myself.

All the mentors Rafael mentions in his story—Caleb, Tracy, and Mark (the Navy Seal)—were part of our Christ Journey church family. Each of them shared encouragement, inspiration, instruction, course corrections, and challenges with him during a mission critical time in his life.

I am very appreciative of Pastor Ralph and others like him who are willing to share so honestly the potential challenges and pitfalls of adolescence. His story is a reminder that adolescence can be a time of turbulence, of testing, of trial, and of training. It's also an assurance of God's continual presence and availability to help us through those difficult years, and if we are willing to turn to Him, adolescence can become a time of triumph!

Spiritual Adolescence

It makes sense that if the purpose of biological adolescence is to help prepare us for the challenges of facing biological adulthood—much like boot camp prepares soldiers for the battles ahead—then spiritual adolescence should serve to prepare us to face the challenges of spiritual adulthood. Spiritual adolescence is when God equips each of us with what we need to become an overcomer in the spiritual struggles we are certain to experience.

Jesus tried to prepare His disciples for future battles. He told them bluntly, "In this world you will have trouble. But take heart! I have overcome the world" (John 16:33). During our adolescent years we quickly discover that physical transformation is not easy. Neither is spiritual transformation. It is full of challenges. And when confronted with some of life's more demanding challenges, such as those that Pastor Ralph shared—we start asking hard questions. One that almost everyone struggles with is, "Why do righteous people suffer while the wicked prosper? What kind of world are we living in?"

In fact, one of the men I've mentored through the years asked me about that recently. I told him I often think about what Jesus said: "Wide is the gate and broad is the road that leads to destruction, and many enter through it. But small is the gate and narrow the road that leads to life, and only a few find it (Matthew 7:13-14). I told my friend that, in my experience, the narrow road runs right up the middle of the broad road that's leading to destruction, but it runs the *opposite* way, against the traffic.

When you start to follow Jesus, it's like you do an immediate about-face and begin to travel against the current. Following the narrow road is like a salmon swimming upstream. The whole force of world culture is rushing downstream, and you've never realized the strength of the current because frankly, you were just going with the flow with the rest of the crowd. But once you turn around and start upstream, it feels like everything is coming against you. However, like the salmon, you have a sense of purpose that makes the effort worth it. Downstream leads to destruction, but following Jesus leads to personal growth and spiritual development. One of the things we learn as spiritual adolescents is that any dead fish can float downstream, but it takes a live one to swim upstream against the strong current of the culture.

Spiritual adolescence is a period of learning what it means *to live upstream in a downstream world.*

Spiritual adolescence is a period of learning what it means *to live upstream in a downstream world*. It's a time of fight, a time of fire, a time when you realize the costs are steep. This is the time to discover, to develop, and then deploy your spiritual weapons . . . your spiritual arsenal.

Adventures in Adolescence

So, what are some indicators that you may be in your spiritual adolescence? One of the first will be a surge in your spirit life that leads you to want more—to grow more and to do more for God. Despite any opposition, you're willing to place yourself at risk to see it happen. Think of the young people in Scripture whose spiritual adolescence was on track with their physical growth:

David

The youngest of eight brothers, David was expected to stay home and run errands while several of his older brothers went off to join the army and fight the Philistines. But when no one in the entire Israelite army was willing to stand up to the giant Goliath, David alone went out to face him. In Goliath's estimation, David was "little more than a boy" (maybe fifteen at the time), but David showed him what an adolescent could do (1 Samuel 17).

Shadrach, Meshach, and Abednego

Three young Israelites, chosen for their physical potential and mental acuity, were taken to Babylon after Jerusalem fell. God gave them exceptional knowledge and understanding of all kinds, and they rose to high positions in the kingdom. But when the pagan King Nebuchadnezzar commanded everyone to bow before an enormous gold statue (the supreme cultural idol of their day), the three young men stood tall as everyone else in the kingdom kneeled. Even when given a second chance and threatened with a dire warning, they refused to bow and were thrown into a super-heated fiery furnace. After God delivered them unharmed, a decree was made forbidding anyone to say anything against their God . . . *and* they all got promotions (Daniel 1, 3).

Esther

Just as a vicious and evil man named Haman was setting out to annihilate every Jew in the kingdom of Persia, a young Jewish woman found herself the new queen of the kingdom. Esther had wisely not revealed her nationality, yet one day she discovered she was the only person who could save her people. Risking her own life, she appealed to the king, thinking, *If I perish, I perish* (Esther 4:16). But King Xerxes supported her, and her courageous action was quickly followed by a clever strategy that exposed (and eventually executed) the hateful Haman. (Although God is never mentioned in Esther's story, His hand is evident in every stage.)

Jesus' disciples

Did you know that Jesus' twelve disciples were most likely *all* in their biological adolescence when He called them to follow Him? Jesus would mentor them and disciple them to become overcomers in the kingdom. They would be the first to comprehend the spiritual truths He was revealing and were the ones Jesus prepared to lead the advance of His kingdom after He returned to the Father.

In the previous chapter we saw Jesus, at age twelve, in the early stages of His own adolescence and beginning to emerge into God's call for His life. He was defining His identity as His Father's Son, choosing His community among wise sages in the Word, and accepting His destiny by confirming, "I must be in my Father's house." It was a period of clarity and discovery. The next time we see Him in Scripture, He's thirty years old and ready to begin His public ministry.

It's important to note that Jesus didn't just plunge from early adolescence to adulthood, from the temple in Jerusalem to the wilderness to be tested. No. Eighteen years of His life—including His adolescence—are unaccounted for in the Bible, although the final two verses of Luke 2 provide some informative clues: "Then he returned to Nazareth with [his parents] and was obedient to them. And his mother stored all these things in her heart. Jesus grew in wisdom and in stature and in favor with God and all the people" (Luke 2:51-52 NLT).

Twelve-year-old Jesus had just astounded all the scholars in the temple, but immediately afterward He submitted to His parents. He was obedient to being taught at home. Don't miss the fact that Jesus *grew* in wisdom, stature, favor with God, and favor with others. This observation is crucial in understanding that adolescence—the time between receiving care as a child and then facing challenges as an adult—is necessarily a time of *growth*. It's when the discoveries we began to make as spiritual preteens are further investigated and developed.

Stepping into Your Warrior

During adolescence we need to avoid all the senseless risky behaviors that can lead to addictions, arrests, or other problems. And yet we also begin to see lots of things that are wrong in the world and need to be made right. We wonder if we should risk getting involved in some of them. There are spiritual battles to be fought; there are victories to be won in virtually every vocational field. God intends some of those battles and victories to be yours.

There are spiritual battles to be fought; there are victories to be won in virtually every vocational field. God intends some of those battles and victories to be yours.

I like to call this period of growth and development *stepping into your warrior*. Biological adolescence is the time where your brain and your body are going through changes to help prepare you for the challenges of being an adult. *Spiritual* adolescence is when you experience growth spurts of faith that that begin to prepare you to become an overcomer when faced with the challenges of life as a spiritual adult.

When John wrote his first letter to the church, he addressed several different groups. Take a look:

I am writing to you, dear children, because your sins have been forgiven on account of his name. I am writing to you, fathers, because you know him who is from the beginning. I am writing to you, young men, because you have overcome the evil one. I write to you, dear children, because you know the Father. I write to you, fathers, because you know him who is from the beginning.

I write to you, young men, because you are strong, and the word of God lives in you, and you have overcome the evil one. (1 John 2:12-14)

You'll find references to three general stages of growth here, each mentioned twice:

Dear children

This group refers to those who have established a personal relationship with the Father and whose sins have been forgiven in His name. I think "children" can refer to the first four stages we covered: Newborn, Infant, Toddler, and Child. Of course, the relationship continues throughout all the stages, so "children" can also refer to *all* believers (for example, 1 John 2:1; 3:7; 4:4; 5:21), but the early stages are where it begins.

Fathers

In our context, this group includes both men and women who have cultivated a deep knowledge of our God who is from the beginning, an understanding of the God who supersedes time. "Fathers" are sages in the spirit. I believe this category correlates with the final three stages on our chart: Parent, Grandparent and Godparent.

Young men

I believe John is referring to all spiritual warriors, both male and female, who are strong in God's truth. The Word of God lives in them and they have overcome the evil one. On our chart, that includes stages 5 through 7: Preteen, Adolescent, and Adult. They are what I call *warrior* stages. You grow during your adolescence by stepping into your warrior.

The Apostle Paul confirmed what John was teaching. In a letter to Timothy, Paul challenged the young pastor: "You then, my son, be strong in the grace that is in Christ Jesus. And the things you have heard me say in the presence of many witnesses entrust to reliable people who will also be qualified to teach others" (2 Timothy 2:1-2). As he continued, Paul challenged Timothy to endure hardships as a soldier trying to please his commanding officer . . . to compete like an athlete observing the rules to avoid being eliminated . . . to work hard and be patient like a farmer waiting for the crops to come in (2 Timothy 2:3-7). These are all challenges to be addressed and disciplines to be learned in the Adolescent stage.

But in his letter to the church in Ephesus, Paul gets specific about the intensity of the spiritual battle all believers fight, and he describes the equipment required to step into our warrior. Here's his checklist of items needed for protection and eventual victory:

Be strong in the Lord and in his mighty power. Put on the full armor of God, so that you can take your stand against the devil's schemes. For our struggle is not against flesh and blood, but against the rulers, against the authorities, against the powers of this dark world and against the spiritual forces of evil in the heavenly realms. Therefore put on the full armor of God, so that when the day of evil comes, you may be able to stand your ground, and after you have done everything, to stand. Stand firm then, with the belt of truth buckled around your waist, with the breastplate of righteousness in place, and with your feet fitted with the readiness that comes from the gospel of peace. In addition to all this, take up the shield of faith, with which you can extinguish all the flaming arrows of the evil one. Take the helmet of salvation and the sword of the Spirit, which is the word of God. (Ephesians 6:10-17)

Astronauts would never think of entering space without a spacesuit, which is especially designed to protect them from temperature extremes, supply them with oxygen and water, and keep them from being injured.

Wise warriors never enter the battlefield without being suited up in their armor. For us, spiritual armor is essential for survival and victory.

Wise warriors never enter the battlefield without being suited up in their armor.

The helmet of salvation is the hope by which we conquer despair and discouragement—the confidence that no matter what happens to you in this life, your eternal relationship with God is sure and certain. The breastplate of righteousness is protection for the attacks of guilt and shame against the heart. The firm footwear of the gospel (like wearing football cleats or golf spikes to maintain secure footing) ensures that you're not slip-sliding away in confusion. God's truth is like a belt that holds everything else in place. The shield of faith is an extra layer of protection in front of you or lifted over you to deflect the flaming arrows of intentional fear that the enemy wants to inflict. (A Roman shield was large enough to protect a soldier's whole body from incoming attacks.) And the sword of the Spirit is the Word of God by which we slice through the enemy's territory, setting the captives free. We do battle with God's authority; we are not limited to our own wisdom and strength.

In previous stages of spiritual growth, you've already learned to clothe yourself, but as an adolescent you regularly suit up in this spiritual armor because the struggles become harder, the battles fiercer. Without the equipment God provides, you find yourself exposed and vulnerable to all kinds of temptations and problems.

Spiritual adolescence is a time of transformation, of rapid and extreme change. To this point in your growth process, the Word of God has been regular sustenance to feed your soul, first as spiritual milk when you were an infant, and later as a solid. But now, as an adolescent, you're starting to confront more dangers in the world and you discover that the Word of God is also the sword of the Spirit. In addition to all your protective armor, you'll need your sword.

Where's the Meat?

In my own experience *as* a spiritual adolescent and after working with many others through the years, I know that many possess a deep hunger for more of God and more of the things of God. They sense there is more than they have experienced, and they want to know where to find it. In the 80s, Wendy's aired a popular series of television commercials, and in each one, actress Clara Peller demands, "Where's the beef?!" (You can watch them on YouTube.) I hear the same urgency in hungry spiritual adolescents who want to know, in terms of their growing faith, "Where's the meat?" I often hear this desire when people complain to me, "Pastor, I'm tired of milk. I know spiritual babies need it, but I need more. When will you feed us some real meat?"

At spiritual adolescence—at warrior stage— Jesus says there's a new diet of *doing*.

At this point in our development, Jesus has a surprise for us. He tells us: "My meat is to do the will of him that sent me, and to finish his work" (John 4:34 KJV). Do you see what He's saying? At spiritual adolescence—at warrior stage—Jesus says there's a new diet of *doing*. The true meat that nourishes growth at this level isn't simply found in a study or a book or even in greater Bible knowledge. It's found in engaging in the field of conflict, in pursuing the *doing* of God's will. Hungry spiritual adolescents face the temptation of eating more Bible content without putting it into practice by doing God's will. As a result, they get fatter but not more spiritually fit. Here's the point: Don't get fat by eating without exercising. Get fit by following Jesus in fulfilling your mission! It's time for action!

In biological teens, emotion and passion spike at this stage for a reason: they have to let it *out;* they *have to* put it into action. The same thing is true for spiritual teenagers. It's time to start *acting* on your faith, not just studying it. At this stage we begin to see why it was so important to learn the lessons of the previous stages, because you can't build an overcoming life from a posture of disobedience. Some people wonder, "Why am I stuck? Why am I stalled?" Let me repeat myself: *You can't build an overcoming life from a posture of disobedience.* We must learn and build on the lessons so far before we can step out and put them into action as we engage the enemy. "Faith without works is dead" (James 2:17). Adolescence is the time you become an action figure with active faith!

God wants you to know that where you've been is simply not enough. When you begin to realize it for yourself, it's time for more. What does "more" look like? Well, we all face at least three possible options. The first is rebellion. You can say, "Nope. No more for me. I'm going to live my life my way." This was the option taken by the younger brother in Jesus' story of the Prodigal Son. He dishonored his father and went and did his own thing, but it didn't work out as he had hoped and planned.

Our second option is "more me"—to get all self-righteous and resist growing in faith and moving forward, and instead convince ourselves that we're just fine, thank you very much! This was the response of the Prodigal Son's older brother. He never left home in a huff, but he stayed home feeling bitter, entitled, and better than his brother. He started feeding his self-righteousness, blaming his father and whining: "You know, you never gave *me* a fatted calf, not even a goat." It's a dead-end option. The older brother demonstrates what my experience has taught me: self-righteousness contains much more *self* than *righteousness*! In other words, we become self-absorbed. But before we denigrate the older brother too harshly, we need to be sure *we're* not too quick to legalistically judge and condemn others as we polish our own halos and think, *I'm so thankful I'm not like that!*

But our third option is "more of God." We begin to suspect there's much more to God and our faith than we've realized so far. In response, don't just *go* through that stage, *grow* through it. Step into your warrior and get into the battle. Enter the danger zone of spiritual service and warfare. Stop merely eating and talking. Start applying and practicing your faith in ways that make a difference. That's your mission from God!

Start applying and practicing your faith in ways that make a difference. That's your mission from God!

Moving On

If you believe you may be in the stage of spiritual adolescence, what can you do to grow today? How do you rise to the next level of spiritual development? Or maybe you're trying to help someone else take those next steps and you want to help them break through whatever has been holding them back. How do you rise to the next level of spiritual development?

To begin with, you need a spiritual mentor. Find a believer who consistently demonstrates strong faith and spiritual maturity. You'll need somebody to love you, listen to you, and lead you. Your mentor is a coach. He or she can encourage you and nudge you to keep moving forward, but can't (and shouldn't) do the work for you. If you're not feeling the fire in your belly to keep growing and doing more for God, it may be time to take a personal inventory of your spiritual life. Review the previous stages and evaluate your progress. Have the lessons become a lifestyle? Or are you a "hearer of the word" but not a "doer of the word"? All progress follows a process. You may not be at the adolescent stage yet, but don't let disobedience be the cause of any lack of progress. A mentor can help you with self-reflection and course corrections, as well as encourage you to take the next steps in your growth. Your mentor will pray that a fresh fire from God will fall on you and produce an authentic spiritual breakthrough!

A mentor will work with you to help you develop in the following areas:

Time

Spending time with your mentor or coach will enable you to develop trust and guidance, and you'll also learn to devote more "alone time" to spiritual disciplines of Bible study, prayer, and so forth. You can always find some other way to fill your time, but spiritual growth must become a priority. A mentor will challenge you to be more intentional with your reading and studying of Scripture, and will also help you discover new opportunities to apply what you're learning. A mentor can introduce you to the six ways of receiving God's Word into your life: hearing (Romans 10:17), reading (Acts 8:28), studying (Acts 17:11), memorizing (Psalm 119:11), meditating (Psalm 1:2) and applying it (James 1:22; Matthew 7:24; John 13:17).

Training

As the two of you meet regularly, your mentor will help you learn to develop your GPS—your Gifts, Passions, and Skills. Until you have a good understanding of how God has gifted you and what you really want to do for Him, it may not do a lot of good to suit up in your spiritual armor and go running toward the battlefield. Work with a ministry leader to find out how your GPS matches a ministry opportunity. Do the groundwork, and then move on to the next area.

Trial and error

This is when you get into the field and try out what you believe. Faith becomes action, no longer just a cognitive exercise. You try out your gifts in service, in ministry, and in outreach, learning as you do. You step into the danger zone, knowing that you risk an encounter with your own version of a fuming giant, a fiery furnace, a hate-filled adversary, or any number of other threats like those we read about in Scripture. Yet regardless of what might happen, your faith keeps you moving forward.

Team

You're never alone in this process. Your mentor should be a solid and reliable support for you, yet you should also have others you touch base with regularly. Your small group, your close friends, and other trusted mature adults will become your second family—brothers and sisters in the Spirit who are fellow warriors with you.

Your mentor can help you through those four important Ts. But there is one more that you must do on your own if you want to keep growing from this point on. No one else will be able to help you. That quality is *Teachability*. If you're not willing to learn, if you're not willing to change, then you won't. If you don't want to grow as an adult, you'll remain stuck and stagnating (and most likely frustrated) at one of the previous stages. But if you come to Jesus with a teachable spirit, you have a curious and humble heart, and you keep learning as a disciple in progress, He has even greater things ahead for you (John 14:12).

STAGE	LESSON
Godparent	
Grandparent	
Parent	
Adult	

Adolescent	Develop. Suit up in spiritual armor, step into your spiritual warrior, and join the battle.
Preteen	Discover who you are: your identity in Christ, where you belong, and your destiny in fulfilling God's will.
Child	Put knowledge into action. Obey God in active faith.
Toddler	Learn to walk in faith and talk to God in prayer as you grow in community with God and others.
Infant	Receive nourishing care from your loving heavenly Father and other spiritual "parents" who want to help you grow.
Newborn	Be born again and receive God's wonderful new life.

In the first three stages, the young believer was saying "feed me." In the next three stages, she was saying "equip me" for a wonderful, effective, God-honoring future. Now, in the rest of the book, we'll see that mature believers are dedicated to help others grow in their faith; they're telling them "follow me."

ADVENTURE PAGES

Pilot's Flight Plan

1. What was one of the biggest challenges you remember about going through your biological adolescence? What did you learn that you can apply to this stage of spiritual adolescence?

2. Review the "armor of God" (below) that Paul described. Which item are you most confident of and comfortable with? Which piece(s) could use a little more attention before you go into your next battle?

   ➤ Salvation (the helmet)

➤ Righteousness (the breastplate)

➤ Truth (the belt)

➤ Peace (the footwear)

➤ Faith (the shield)

➤ Knowledge of the Word of God (the sword)

3. When you find yourself spiritually stuck, do you tend to rebel? To become self-righteous? Or to grow through the stalled period? Explain your answer.

4. How do you feel to be at a stage that will begin to involve more risk on your part? Why?

5. How would you explain to someone what it means to "step into your warrior"? Have you done that (or are you ready to) so you can move on to the next stage?

Course Correction

If you only do one thing, do this: Take some time to imagine putting on each piece of spiritual armor, and then imagine yourself as God's warrior in your current struggles in life.

Captain's Log

If you're helping a spiritual adolescent grow, I suggest:

➤ Be patient . . . very patient. Realize that this stage often has many ups and downs.

➤ Impart a vision of the person's impact. Discuss strengths, desires, and gifting, and paint a picture of how God might use him or her in the future.

➤ Good mentors, like good parents, give those they care for "roots and wings." Provide plenty of support and security, but also, encourage creativity and courage.

ADULTING YOUR LIFE

ADULT

"I'm starting with the man in the mirror . . .
if you want to make the world a better place
take a look at yourself then make a change."

—"Man in the Mirror," Michael Jackson

What does it mean to become an adult? It all depends on whom you ask . . . and perhaps on where you live. Throughout the world, celebrations to acknowledge "becoming a man" or "becoming a woman" are numerous and varied. Some are casual and informal, like Sweet 16 parties for girls in the U.S. Others, like the Quinceañera for fifteen-year-old girls in Latin America, are more culturally traditional, accompanied by feasts for the guests. Some celebrations are more overtly religious, like Jewish Bar Mitzvahs and Bat Mitzvahs. Japan has an annual "Coming-of-Age Day" to celebrate and honor everyone—young men and women—who turned twenty during the year, enabling them to legally drink, smoke, and vote.

Some cultures, however, have more challenging requirements. The Apache Sunrise Ceremony is a four-day, physically taxing rite to acknowledge that a girl is becoming a woman. The girl is literally painted with a mixture of cornmeal and clay that she must not wash off until the end of the ceremony. Like many native-American rites of passage, this one involves family and community in acknowledging the young person's rise to adulthood, and emphasizes the tribe's longstanding traditions and heritage.[16]

A death-defying ritual from the island of Vanuatu requires a boy to strap one leg to a vine atop a wooden platform that might be up to one hundred feet off the ground. His mother stands beside him with an item from his childhood. She throws it off the platform as he leaps, with the goal of stopping as close to the ground as possible. If he touches the ground, the tribe expects a good harvest.

Then again, if you want to become a man in one Brazilian Amazon tribe, you go out and collect a lot of bullet ants—the most powerful biting ants in the world—to bring back to a tribal elder so he can sew them into woven gloves. You then wear the gloves for ten minutes at a time for at least twenty times over the next several weeks. If you can avoid the paralysis that occasionally results, you pass the initiation and are an adult.[17] (I think I'll pass.)

Adulting

I thought you might like to see how some other cultures handle the process of becoming an adult before we move on to the next stage of our process to become mature-ish. What I'm suggesting in this chapter may not seem so demanding in comparison to other cultures! However, even when we limit our observations to American culture, we're going to see that it's still not a simple matter to determine exactly when we make that eventful transition from child to adult.

So far we've seen that in natural life there is a *process to all progress,* from seed to stem to blossom to fruit. It's the same with human development—from newborn to childhood, through adolescence and adulthood. And now we ask, What does it mean to be a human adult?

From a biological standpoint, the answer seems rather simple. In fact, our family members start to let us know before we even give the matter much thought. They come up to us at family reunions and say things like, "Oh, look at you. You're so grown up!" What they mean is that the physical changes they are beholding leave little doubt that the person before them is no longer just a little boy or little girl.

Maybe you were taught in high school biology that you reach adulthood when your body has the capacity to reproduce, but now experts are saying that the human brain doesn't reach maturity until the mid-twenties or maybe early thirties. So can you truly call yourself an adult before your brain is fully developed? It does seem to verify that you can reproduce before you know what's really going on. It's confusing. But on a positive note, some people believe that human brain development continues in some form throughout all our years, which means there's still hope for all of us.

Our culture adds to our confusion about what constitutes an "adult." When you turn sixteen, you're deemed eligible to get behind the wheel of a car and barrel down the road on your own. That sounds like an acknowledgment of maturity, doesn't it? But it will be two more years before you can vote, enlist in the military without parental consent, or get married in many states. You can't legally consume alcohol until you're twenty-one. However, twenty-five states don't have a minimum marriageable age, which means that if you get married as a teenager and realize it was a mistake, you can't legally drown your sorrows until you're twenty-one. (Bad joke, I know.)

In the twentieth century, the path to adulthood seemed somewhat standardized: find a mate, raise a family, begin an occupation, and run a home. These days it's more complex. Kelly Williams Brown is a writer born in 1984, which means social researchers would call her a Millennial. She's credited with inventing the word *adulting*, referring to actions that comprise maturity, and she wrote a book about it that started a lot of conversations. [18] *Atlantic* magazine ran an article citing her book and asked readers to respond with when they felt they became grownups (if ever). Here are a few of their (edited) responses[19]:

➤ "Being a Millennial and trying to adult is wildly disorienting. I can't figure out if I'm supposed to start a non-profit, get another degree, develop a wildly profitable entrepreneurial venture, or somehow travel the world and make it look effortless online. Mostly it just looks like taking a job that won't ever pay off my student debt in a field that is not the one that I studied. Then, if I hold myself to the traditional ideal of what it means to be an adult, I'm also not nailing it. I am unmarried, and not settled into a long term, financially stable career. . . . It's unfair to judge myself, but I confess I fall into the trap of comparison often enough. Sometimes because I simply desire those things for myself, and sometimes because of Instagram."

➤ "For the last several years, I've felt a pressure—it might be a biological or a social pressure—to get out from under the yoke of my parents' financial assistance. I feel that only when I'm able to support myself financially will I be a true 'adult.' Some of the traditional markers of adulthood (turning 18, turning 21) have come and gone without me feeling any more adult-y, and I don't think that marriage would make me feel grown up unless it was accompanied by financial independence."

➤ "I'm an OB/GYN and watch women struggle through many life changes. . . . I think the answer to 'when do you become an adult' has to do with when you finally have acceptance of yourself. My patients who are trying to stop time through menopause don't seem like adults even though they are in their mid-40s, mid-50s. My patients who seem secure through any of life struggles, those are the women who seem like adults. They still have a young soul but roll with all the changes, accepting the undesirable changes in their bodies, accepting the lack of sleep with their children, accepting the things they cannot change."

➤ "For a long time, I've been waiting for that 'I am an adult' feeling. I am 27 years old, married, living on my own, and employed as a manager at a successful hotel company. I expected all of these things, age, marriage, career, to trigger the feeling. Looking back, I think I was asking the wrong question. I don't think I spent a lot of time as a child or teenager. I have worked since I was 13 and I worked with other kids my age. Our parents were immigrants who made little more than us. We were our families' translators since childhood. Utilities and banks have heard my prepubescent voice as my mother/father/etc. I think for some of us, we reached adulthood before we realized it."

These stories confirm that there's no simple answer to the questions, "When are you really an adult?" And "What does a grownup look like?" In these times we're living in, the lines are blurry, aren't they?

Spiritual Adulting

Let's turn our attention to spiritual maturity at this stage. Perhaps we can arrive at a more satisfying answer if we change the question to, "What does it means to be 'all grown up' *spiritually*?"

That's our focus as Christ-followers at this stage. How can you know, as a person of living faith, that you are spiritually grown up? Did you know in Scripture that becoming and being a spiritual grown up is *never* a matter of chronological age? You can be young in physical years but wise and strong in spiritual adulting. Then again, you can be advanced in calendar years and still be unaware of God's resources for your life, living below your privilege as a child of God, and never really become spiritually mature.

Failure to mature spiritually is a tragedy. God has a vision and potential plan for *every* human being to find fulfillment in Christ. This truth is reinforced throughout Scripture:

➤ "His divine power has given us everything we need for a godly life through our knowledge of him who called us by his own glory and goodness. Through these he has given us his very great and precious promises, so that through them you may participate in the divine nature" (2 Peter 1:3-4).

➤ "I pray that you, being rooted and established in love, may have power, together with all the Lord's holy people, to grasp how wide and long and high and deep is the love of Christ, and to know this love that surpasses knowledge—that you may be filled to the measure of all the fullness of God" (Ephesians 3:17-19).

➤ "Speaking the truth in love, we will grow to become in every respect the mature body of him who is the head, that is, Christ" (Ephesians 4:15).

➤ "Anyone who loves their brother and sister lives in the light, and there is nothing in them to make them stumble" (1 John 2:10).

Look at the benefits of continued spiritual growth piling up in these passages: divine power that provides everything we need, love that surpasses knowledge, filled to all the fullness of God, a Christ-like level of maturity, and the ability to avoid spiritual stumbles. There is so much more to your faith than simply receiving Christ, being born again, and going to heaven! No wonder the author of Hebrews pleads: "Let us move beyond the elementary teachings about Christ and be taken forward to maturity" (Hebrews 6:1). In other words, it's time to grow up!

Being born again is like *starting* your car, but you don't just start it to sit idle in the driveway. Once the car's engine is running, the process of spiritual maturity is *going* places in it. God has sky-high plans for each of His children . . . including you.

In His Sermon on the Mount, Jesus challenged His listeners: "Be perfect . . . as your heavenly Father is perfect" (Matthew 5:48). Does He really intend for us to be as flawless as God? Of course not. But I do think He's telling us we always have a little farther to go on our spiritual journey. There's always a little more room to grow.

As I explained in Stage 1, Jesus is certainly not talking about people obsessing on perfection*ism*, which was what led to the Pharisees' problem with hypocrisy and self-righteousness. That's not what following Christ is about. As Mark Twain once said, "Some people are good in the worst sense of the word." Instead, Jesus wants our faith to become fully grown, completely developed. The goal at each stage of your growth is to become fully developed and to maximize your potential at that stage.

In fact, let's review the central lessons at each stage so far as we have progressed to the Adult stage:

STAGE	LESSON
Godparent	
Grandparent	
Parent	
Adult	Take responsibility for your own spiritual life. Be filled to the whole measure of the fullness of Christ.
Adolescent	Develop. Suit up in spiritual armor, step into your spiritual warrior, and join the battle.
Preteen	Discover who you are: your identity in Christ, where you belong, and your destiny in fulfilling God's will.
Child	Put knowledge into action. Obey God in active faith.
Toddler	Learn to walk in faith and talk to God in prayer as you grow in community with God and others.
Infant	Receive nourishing care from your loving heavenly Father and other spiritual "parents" who want to help you grow.
Newborn	Be born again and receive God's wonderful new life.

And now, as you see, we've arrived at the central lesson for spiritual young adults, which is, in a word, *Responsibility*. This is the stage where you take responsibility for your life under God in Christ. You take responsibility for *doing* the will of God. Spiritual adulting involves more than just learning and thinking and feeling; it requires doing. It's time to put those lessons and thoughts and feelings into practice.

You take responsibility for *doing* the will of God.

Biological adulting involves doing things like going to work, getting married, raising kids, surviving catastrophes, and making a difference in the world. Spiritually, adults have just come through adolescence where they learned to step into their warrior, began to seek first God's kingdom and His righteousness, let God's truth set them free, and learned the strength of community in church and small groups. Those are probably new experiences for a lot of people. But spiritual adults begin to take responsibility for continuing all those things and ensuring that they continue to happen in their lives. As adults, the new experiences become habits.

The New Testament tells us that you're not meant to *be* God, but you are created in the image of God to *belong* to God, to become *like* God, and then to be *filled to the whole measure of the fullness of Christ* (Ephesians 4:13). This is really good news, because it means that nobody can maximize all of their human potentials in this life alone. It takes eternity for that, but in the meantime you *can* fulfill the will of God *for your life*. It starts with praying the prayer Jesus taught us: "Your will be done on earth as it is in heaven." You can bring heaven to earth every day in your personal life. That's what spiritual adults begin to do.

Q & A

As we get farther along in the spiritual growth process, we tend to start asking more questions. Here are five basic questions that keep coming up as I discuss this topic with others. I hope they'll help you better understand this initial plunge into spiritual adulting.

Question #1: How do I know when the Adult phase begins? What does it look like?

You're continuing what you began in the Adolescent stage, and as your trust in God's faithfulness increases, so does your self-confidence. You're suited up for battle, wearing your spiritual armor and beginning to lead a life that engages and overcomes the enemy. You're making him nervous because you're learning to avoid his traps and see through his schemes. You are ready to make decisions that will weaken his influence and strengthen God's kingdom. You're making good decisions, overcoming temptation, and doing the right things. The author of Hebrews says that those who are mature, through training and practice, develop the skill to distinguish good from evil (Hebrews 5:14). Doing the right thing, at the right time, in the right way, for the right reasons, is the way of life for spiritual adults.

In addition, you're Spirit-filled, bearing spiritual fruit, and using your spiritual gifts. (If you haven't yet determined what your gifts are, see Romans 12:4-8, 1 Corinthians 12:4-11, Ephesians 4:11-13, and 1 Peter 4:8-11 for several lists and descriptions). You're yielding to God's Spirit within you, flowing through you like a river of living water (John 7:38). You're demonstrating the fruit of God's Spirit in your life, and other people are noticing your increasing love, joy, peace, patience, kindness, goodness, gentleness, faithfulness, and self-control (Galatians 5:22-23). When people begin spiritually adulting, they stand out in a crowd as their light shines brighter for God. Is that happening in your life?

But if you want one clear indicator that you've become a fully mature and complete spiritual adult, James gives us one of the final obstacles to master in spiritual growth: you can control your tongue. He says, "We all stumble in many ways. Anyone who is never at fault in what they say is perfect, able to keep their whole body in check" (James 3:2). If you are ever able to master your tongue, he says, you are approaching real maturity. For most of us, that's an area we need to improve throughout our lives.

Once again, let's remember that your spiritual progress isn't linked to chronological age. It's not a matter of calendar years. You don't just arrive and then lock it in once for all. It's a dynamic process. Even the Apostle Paul said, "I don't mean to say that I have already achieved these things or that I have already reached perfection. But I press on to possess that perfection for which Christ Jesus first possessed me" (Philippians 3:12 NLT). He's saying, "I haven't yet 'arrived.' I'm still learning. But I'm taking responsibility for my own life under God in Christ." That is the mind-set of a spiritual adult.

Question #2: What's the central lesson of adulting?

In two words: *taking responsibility*. We've seen that during the turbulence of adolescence, you can be your own worst enemy. You have a lot of changes to work through, but in the spiritual adulting stage, taking responsibility shows you that you're becoming your own best friend . . . growing up . . . taking the next step. It was Paul's experience. Immediately after he wrote of pressing on to possess the perfection of Christ, he added: "No, dear brothers and sisters, I have not achieved it, but I focus on this one thing: Forgetting the past and looking forward to what lies ahead, I press on to reach the end of the race and receive the heavenly prize for which God, through Christ Jesus, is calling us" (Philippians 3:13-14 NLT). He adds that it's something all spiritually mature people should agree on and commit to (Philippians 3:15-16).

So, you know you're a spiritual adult when you take full responsibility for your spiritual life. You don't blame somebody else for what's not happening in you. You don't use others as scapegoats for your personal failures and shortcomings. Instead, you keep on keeping on, and you build on where you've been. You fight the battles, and you keep rowing in the storm. Adulthood has many requirements, but they all start with taking responsibility for yourself, for your life, for your choices, and for whatever consequences may result.

We will face strong enemies, yet we need not fear them if we keep growing and stay close to God.

We will face strong enemies, yet we need not fear them if we keep growing and stay close to God. Like warrior David, we can be confident even in the worst of times: "You prepare a table before me in the presence of my enemies. You anoint my head with oil; my cup overflows" (Psalm 23:5).

God gives us the power of choice, as human beings created in His image, but as Christ-followers, God also gives us the power of Jesus' blood for forgiveness and healing. He gives us His Spirit to empower our lives. And He gives us the power of His Word to enable us to align our lives to the truth of His Word and find greater freedom. All His power-producing gifts allow us as spiritual adults to become overcomers in the battles of life.

Question #3: What will I encounter as I engage in battle?

Speaking of battle, that's an image that can be frightening to consider. We're not talking about a fair fight against flesh and blood; our spiritual enemy will try to sneak up on us and create diversions to take us away from God's way and God's will. As soon as Jesus began His public ministry as an adult, He waged spiritual battle in the wilderness, facing the cunning Tempter and three powerful temptations. You'll be tempted, too, facing the same spiritual enemy: the evil one, the liar, the accuser, the deceiver, the master of misdirection, distraction, and destruction.

Seventy-two of the Psalms—almost half—mention enemies. Our enemies aren't only those who oppose us personally, but also include those who oppose God's way of life. If we're not careful, we become our own worst enemies. The Tempter wraps the good gifts of God in lies and then twists them toward self-interest, self-indulgence, and self-determined living. Gradually, self rather than God becomes the center of our lives. We let it happen because our fallen sinful nature already believes that and wants it to be true. We start thinking, *I've got to watch out for #1,* forgetting that back at the Infant stage we agreed that God is #1, not you and me.

When this happens, we've fallen for a lie. It's just one of the many traps and temptations we can fall into. And then, as soon as we mess up or get distracted or are deceived by one of the evil one's traps, he heaps on guilt, shame, blame, fear, and doubt. Next thing you know, you're being tempted to bury those feelings with drugs, alcohol, sex, money, success, lust, power, greed, or anger.

That's why the armor of God matters so much. You can review the individual items in the last chapter (or Ephesians 6:10-17), but remember that it's the belt of truth that holds everything else in place. God's truth is what Jesus used to resist temptation in the wilderness (Matthew 4:1-11), and it's what we need to use too. When you're mugged by temptation, nobody else can fight that battle for you. It's now up to you to take responsibility.

Question #4: How do I grow to become a spiritual overcomer?

You already know the answer to this one. You learned it back in your spiritual childhood, although now, at the spiritual adult level, you're taking more personal responsibility than ever before to apply these truths. In short, the answer is three words: *Believe, Receive,* and *Achieve.* Let's do a quick review.

Believe—You believe God's Word, especially concerning Christ's death and resurrection. As you continue through the stages of spiritual growth, your belief is increasingly demonstrated by your developing trust in God and willing obedience to Him. As an adult, you realize that total obedience to Christ requires no less than a death: "I have been crucified with Christ and I no longer live, but Christ lives in me. The life I now live in the body, I live by faith in the Son of God, who loved me and gave himself for me" (Galatians 2:20). In other words, Paul says, "Jesus didn't just die for me; I died with Him, and I am now dead to sin because of His death, burial, and resurrection." The spiritual battles you fight as an adult include this ongoing battle to let Christ reign supreme in your life, and daily dying to self. Jesus said, "Whoever wants to be my disciple must deny themselves and take up their cross and follow me" (Luke 9:23). When He said that, everyone knew the only reason anyone took up a cross was to die on it.

Receive—Because you no longer live but Christ lives in you, you receive the power of the resurrection in life. God created you as a unique individual, and He gave you special gifts and talents. "Dying to self" doesn't mean you lose all that. My sinful nature died in Christ, but my personality, my individuality, my autonomy is still very present and very real in Christ who lives in me. I'm the glove, but He's the controlling hand. I'm the wire, but He's the power that flows through me into my world. I receive what He provides, and in doing so, I experience fullness in my life because of Christ's life.

Achieve—Only after believing and receiving am I able to achieve the will of God. Only after I allow Christ's faith and love to be expressed in me can I determine and fulfill His will in my life, in my marriage and family, in my vocation, in my career, and in my ministry.

Only after believing and receiving am I able to achieve the will of God.

Question #5: What if I fail? What happens then?

This question isn't, "What happens *if* I fail?" but should really be, "What happens *when* I fail?" It's going to happen. Count on it. Peter was absolutely certain he was willing to die for Christ, but by the next morning, he had denied Him three times (Matthew 26:31-35; 69-75). That was Peter's final memory before Jesus died. But after Jesus' resurrection, He took Peter aside and asked him three times, "Do you love me?" (John 21:15-19). Why? Because Jesus was gently but firmly helping Peter take responsibility for his failure. He was inviting him to step into his spiritual adult. And every time that Peter answered that question, Jesus gave him something to do: feed My lambs; feed My sheep; care for others. That's the focus of spiritual adulting—taking responsibility and *doing* something.

So how does Christ mentor us as spiritual adolescents into our adulthood? He calls us to accept responsibility for our past failures and for our future in doing the will of God because we love Him. As He reminded Peter, a spiritual adult doesn't live only for *himself*. Taking responsibility for our own growth is another step toward becoming a reliable, reproducing leader for somebody else. Maybe that's where God has you today—not just connected in an existing group, but perhaps considering leadership in a new group where you take responsibility not just for yourself, but also in helping others. If so, hold that thought. That sounds like spiritual parenting, which is the stage we'll examine next.

ADVENTURE PAGES

Pilot's Flight Plan

1. When would you say you officially became an adult? What were the circumstances that caused you to arrive at that decision?

2. To what extent have you achieved the stage of spiritual Adult—of taking responsibility for your own faith and ongoing growth?

3. What are some spiritual battles you've faced recently? Do you feel that you were sufficiently equipped with armor and the sword of the Spirit (God's Word) to handle them? If not, what was lacking?

4. What do you think Jesus meant when He said, "Be perfect . . . as your heavenly Father is perfect"?

5. Are you afraid of failing if you take responsibility to step up and attempt new and more challenging things for God? Why? What's the worst that could happen? What's the best that could happen?

Course Correction

If you only do one thing, do this: Write out what's your responsibility (for your spiritual, relational, emotional, and financial health) and what's not.

Captain's Log

If you're helping a spiritual adult grow, I suggest:

➤ One of the most important tasks of adults is to clearly define their responsibilities. Don't make assumptions about what the person you're helping understands in this area. Take the time to list responsibilities . . . and the limits of responsibilities.

➤ Help the person determine the source of conflict and confusion. Is it from the tension between God's calling and the lure of the culture? Is it from bad habits or false assumptions that are deeply embedded in her heart? Or is it genuine spiritual attack? (In most cases, it's a combination of all three!)

➤ For many people, failure is traumatic. They can't "just blow it off" because to them, it demonstrates they are defective. If the person's reaction is out of proportion to the event, explore that perception and feeling, and reemphasize the message of God's great love and grace.

STAGE EIGHT

RE-FRESHING
THE DEAD SEA

PARENT

"It's never too late to have a happy childhood."

—Randall Wallace, author of *Braveheart*

As a freshman at Northern Arizona University, I took a class titled Introduction to Education. One of my assignments was to write a paper about the most significant person in my life. I decided to write about Jesus Christ, who had recently changed my life profoundly—how I met Him, how I had experienced freedom from guilt to discover a new purpose and new peace in my life, and why He's the most significant person in my life as my Savior and Lord. The day our professor was returning those papers, he said, "I want a couple of you to read your paper out loud to the class." He first called the name of another student, and then he said, "Mr. White, you can be the second."

Suddenly I got scared. I guess I was afraid of being rejected or ridiculed. Even remembering that day makes my palms a little sweaty right now. But I started praying a verse I had memorized: "I am not ashamed of the gospel of Christ: for it is the power of God unto salvation to every one that believes" (Romans 1:16). I just kept repeating the verse to myself until my professor called on me, and then I read what I had written about my life experience in Christ. The classroom was very quiet. When I finished, he simply said, "Thank you." There was no discussion.

But when class was over, a friend of mine named Toby came over and asked, "Can I have a copy of what you just read? I've never heard anything like that. I'd like to read it to my parents." I had simply written what it was like to receive the love and forgiveness of Jesus, how I was learning to pray, and how it made me feel. Now Toby was going to read that to his family. Do you know what God was teaching me? Looking back, that moment may have been my first experience with becoming a spiritual parent . . . advancing to the next stage of my spiritual journey. Maybe you haven't realized it yet, but God now wants to help you grow in giving His life to others.

> Maybe you haven't realized it yet,
> but God now wants to help you grow
> in giving His life to others.

Ezekiel Takes a Swim

One of the highlights of any trip to Israel is visiting the Dead Sea. It's the lowest elevation on earth at 1,412 feet below sea level. It's also one of the world's saltiest bodies of water—nine times saltier than the ocean. Our tour group loved wading in and bobbing around on the surface because the water is so salty that almost anything floats in it.

Why is it called a "Dead" Sea? Two reasons. First, it's so low that whatever flows in can't get out, so it's a dead end of the flow of water. And second, it is so salty that nothing can live in it. In some ways, the Dead Sea as a clear symbol of people living with no acknowledgment of God. No spiritual life. No eternal life for sure. In fact, "dead" is exactly the word

Scripture uses to describe our lives before we are born again and are made new by receiving His life in Christ.

The Bible says that you and I, when we followed the ways of this world apart from Christ, were *dead* in our transgressions and sins . . . our trespasses and missteps . . . our deliberate rebellion . . . our selfish acts (Ephesians 2:1-2). When it came to knowing God—feeling, hearing, sensing God—we were deaf, blind, and hardhearted. We were dead. Flat-lining. And people who are dead certainly have no expectation or means of experiencing *eternal* life. This truth applies not only to you, but also to your spouse, your girlfriend or boyfriend, your husband or wife, your mom and dad, your children, your friends, your boss, and every person you know who is biologically alive. Spiritual death is a pandemic much more prevalent and devastating than COVID-19. Many people are living "Dead Sea lives" and desperately need new life! I was dead, but I didn't know it until I met the Lord.

If the Dead Sea is a symbol of life apart from God, what's the opposite? What symbol captures and communicates life immersed in and flowing full with God's life? There's a fantastic vision found in Ezekiel 47 that paints the picture for us. During his lifetime, the prophet Ezekiel had several powerful visions. In this one, he was accompanied by a heavenly guide with a measuring rod (Ezekiel 40:1-4). The angel had been measuring the various rooms in a temple, and when he led Ezekiel outside, the prophet saw a great flow of water pouring out from under the temple to create a river. The angel used his measuring rod to mark off 1000 long cubits (1750 feet) and walked into the river with Ezekiel to that point, where the water was ankle deep. Another thousand cubits in, the water was knee deep. After another thousand, it was up to Ezekiel's waist. After yet another thousand (putting him 7000 feet—well over a mile—out into the river), the water was not only deep enough to swim in, it had become a river no one could cross.

The angelic guide asked Ezekiel, "Son of man, do you see this?" (Ezekiel 47:6) In other words, "This is important. You don't want to miss it!" When the two returned to the riverbank, Ezekiel noticed groves of fruit trees growing on both sides of the river. The angel explained that the water from the sanctuary enabled the trees to bear fruit of all kinds throughout the year, and the trees would provide both food and healing.

In addition, "Swarms of living creatures will live wherever the river flows. There will be large numbers of fish, . . . where the river flows everything will live." Even better was *where* this river will be flowing and what will be the results. Ezekiel was told, "This water flows toward the eastern region and goes down into the Arabah [the Jordan Valley running south from the Sea of Galilee], *where it enters the Dead Sea.* When it empties into the sea, the salty water there becomes *fresh*" (Ezekiel 47:8-9, emphasis added).

Ezekiel had been specifically instructed to "look carefully and listen closely and pay attention to everything" and to "tell the people of Israel everything you see" (Ezekiel 40:4). Yet this grand vision wasn't just for Israel thousands of years ago. It's for you, for me, and for all of us.

Your Dead-Sea life is so complicated, so deadened by sin, that everything seems lifeless and hopeless. But it's not. There's another river from a very different source: the presence of a loving, forgiving God. The river of the water of life from God is flowing, making everything new and fresh, overwhelming death and sin and their influence on you. It makes you vibrantly alive to bear life and share life!

The Living and the Dead

So, let me ask you the question Ezekiel was asked: "Do you see this?" Lots of people miss it. Spiritually dead people roam our world today like zombies—busy, but oblivious to meaning, life, hope, and joy—but Jesus wants us all to become fully alive. He said, "Let anyone who is thirsty come to me and drink. Whoever believes in me, as Scripture has said, rivers of living water will flow from within them" (John 7:37-38). In this passage, the word for *rivers* means "torrents; rushing mighty streams."

In His next sentence, Jesus made it clear that He was talking about the Holy Spirit bringing life and then flowing and growing through believers as a channel of God's life to the world.

Now let's couple that thought with something else Jesus said to His disciples shortly after His resurrection: "As the Father has sent me, I am sending you" (John 20:21).

What do you call people who (1) bring life to others who never had life before, and (2) prepare and train them to act independently in the world to eventually carry on in their place? I believe Jesus is both defining and modeling the job description of a *parent*—a spiritual parent.

So far, we've moved through seven stages to reach spiritual adulthood, but I suspect there may be some protests at this point. Some readers may be thinking: *I've tracked with you so far because I can relate to all those stages. But now you're losing me because I've never been a parent in the biological sense.*

You bring up a good point. Everyone who grows into a full-grown *biological* adult first is a newborn, infant, toddler, child, preteen, and adolescent. But not every adult becomes a parent, grandparent, or godparent. However, spiritual development supersedes biological development at this point because everyone can continue to grow through all the *spiritual* stages. In fact, spiritual growth demands that we continue beyond the Adult stage. Up to this point, we've been almost entirely focused on our own individual spiritual growth. Oh, we've mentioned the importance of community and mentors and outside influencers, but the emphasis has been on your personal growth, not theirs.

Here's where we make a shift. We go out into this spiritually dead world to share the source of life, and we begin to invest the things we've learned into the lives of "young" believers who are in the earlier stages. What's the difference between being a spiritual adult and a spiritual parent? Both grow to maturity, but the parent also turns his or her attention to another generation of spiritual children.

From here forward, we stop making further biological comparisons and start speaking entirely of spiritual growth, even though we do so in a context of family life (remembering that "family" can extend far beyond flesh-and-blood relations).

You will let God use you to help someone else find and follow Christ.

If you want to keep growing into your full, God-given potential in Christ, you will move through the Adult stage into spiritual parenting. You will let God use you to help someone else find and follow Christ. Lots of people tinker around with faith and spiritual growth, but a reliable spiritual parent can be hard to find. When Paul wrote the dysfunctional church in Corinth, he reminded them: "Even if you had ten thousand guardians in Christ, you did not have many fathers, for in Christ Jesus I became your father through the gospel. Therefore, I urge you to imitate me" (1 Corinthians 4:15-16). Paul is saying the Corinthians were born again by God's choice through him. In other words, "I am your spiritual daddy!"

A Job Too Big?

The first call that Jesus gave His disciples was, "Come, follow me, and I will send you out to fish for people" (Matthew 4:19). The last call He gave them was, "Go and make disciples of all nations, baptizing them in the name of the Father and of the Son and of the Holy Spirit, and teaching them to obey everything I have commanded you" (Matthew 28:19). Both of those are calls to become spiritual parents. He was encouraging His followers to look beyond their own concerns and spiritual growth, and in doing so, He promised to show them how to live a life larger than themselves. He wanted them to see that they could become a life-giving channel of salvation to others.

Two thousand years later, this is still God's plan for our Dead-Sea world. Look around. Do you see a lot of people living abundant spiritual lives? Or do you see a Dead-Sea planet populated by people with Dead-Sea lives, Dead-Sea relationships, Dead-Sea stagnant marriages, and Dead-Sea dead-end legalistic or moralistic religion? People apart from God. Dead in their trespasses. Stuck in their past mistakes.

Have you ever cried out for God to bring new life to the spiritually dead people in your family? Your home? Your neighborhood? Your city? Your country? And your world? Do you wonder if God has a plan to reach all those people? After all, you say, it's going to take a long time to change the world.

Yes, God has a plan . . . and you're already experiencing it. How did *you* come to know the light and truth of God while living in your Dead-Sea world? Isn't it because somebody, at some point, cared enough to pray for you, to stay with you, to listen to you, and to love you? Didn't someone share their story of how they received God's love in Christ and trusted Him for the forgiveness of sin, turning from their selfish dead ways and allowing His Spirit to come alive in them? By the way, that's what water baptism by immersion represents: a burial of our Dead-Sea mentalities and a rising to new life to begin a thriving, growing relationship with God.

God's plan is not to instantaneously bring the life-giving water of His Spirit to everyone in our Dead-Sea world with one sweep of His mighty hand. He doesn't do it through secular education, government, elections, demonstrations, or even social media posts. God's plan is to do it life-on-life, one at a time. He uses people to build personal bridges of relationship that allow His life to flow to the people around us. He changes the world by changing you.

So far, we've looked at how He changes you through all the stages from Newborn to Child to Adult. Now it's time to become a spiritual

Parent to others. It's the next step in growing into more of your God-given potential.

A Deeper Experience

Let's consider Ezekiel's vision again. He shows us an amazing, miraculous rush of water flowing from the temple of God, and wherever it flows, it gives life. That river is still flowing—but rather than water, the river is now the Holy Spirit. And rather than a physical building, the temple from which the Holy Spirit flows is . . . you. Paul reminds us: "Do you not know that your bodies are temples of the Holy Spirit, who is in you, whom you have received from God?" (1 Corinthians 6:19)

Your life now is that channel where the river flows. The river is a symbol of your growth and ongoing spiritual maturity as you continue to move out into deeper water:

Ankle deep

You're beginning to walk in the Spirit. This is what we start learning to do during our series of foundational childhood stages. You don't go anywhere with God without learning how to walk in the Spirit. We don't move ahead until we learn to keep in step with the Spirit (Galatians 5:25). This is what faithful obedience is all about.

Knee deep

This is daily praying in fellowship with the Holy Spirit. We learn how to follow God's promptings in our daily conversations, and to pray that His will might be done on earth as it is in heaven. As we move into spiritual adolescence and adulthood, this means putting on our spiritual armor and moving forward with His power in us as we approach the battlefield. Immediately after Paul lists the items of spiritual armor, he instructs: "And pray in the Spirit on all occasions with all kinds of prayers and requests. With this in mind, be alert and always keep on praying for all the Lord's people" (Ephesians 6:18). First, we put on all the armor of God. Next, we pray that God's kingdom will advance as His will is done on earth as it is in heaven. And then His Spirit can flow through us to bring life to others.

Waist deep

This is where spiritual adults become spiritual parents. It's a point of spiritual reproduction. It's when you learn to love others enough to inter-act with them, listen to them, and allow the Holy Spirit to help you know how to share your faith and when to apply the gospel story to their point of need so they can pray, receive God's life, and come alive in Him. Has anybody come alive in Christ yet because of you? Warrior believer, have you given birth by God's grace to other warriors in the making? Are you inspiring new overcomers by sharing the hope that God has given you?

Sometimes we think, *Oh, they're not interested. They're just too hard-hearted.* Or, *There are just too many obstacles in their way right now.* Or maybe, *I don't have confidence I can answer all the questions—and I'm sure they'll be really hard questions.* Listen, sister or brother, nothing is too hard for God. As you continue to mature, you'll realize that people are far from God in this world. They're in the dark. They're living Dead-Sea lives, so it's unrealistic for them to have or meet freshwater expectations. But that should never stop us from letting the fresh water of God's Spirit flow from us to them in a way that enables them to experience life and growth. "How beautiful are the feet of those who bring good news!" (Romans 10:14-15)

Full immersion

Notice that Ezekiel was prompted to keep going until he found him-self in water deep enough to swim in . . . far enough to realize there was no way to cross the powerful river. This was the point where his angelic guide asked him, "Do you see this?" As God's Spirit keeps flowing through us and filling us, we lose our fears and inhibitions about reaching out to oth-ers. Seeing how God works, and sharing in the experience of parenting others, is like a refreshing swim on a sweltering day. (We'll take another look at Ezekiel in the deep water in Stage 10.)

Critics and Other Obstacles

So far, we have been following the stages of spiritual growth and maturity, but clearly, not everyone chooses to go through those stages. Some people never want to have anything to do with God. More frequently, though, someone will start through the process and eventually reach a point where he loses interest, becomes discouraged, rebels, or simply becomes unwilling to commit to further growth.

In thinking about this and all the conversations I've had throughout the years with people who have not yet met Christ, I created a list to differentiate some of the reasons they resist spiritual growth. These aren't hardline categories, but they are stages of unbelief that I have witnessed:

➤ Spiritually Apathetic—When it comes to the things of God, some people have a hardness of heart that leaves them unfeeling and uncaring. I was there myself for a while.

➤ Hostile Atheist—"Hostile" may be too strong a word, but perhaps you've met people who insist there is no God, and they seem to go out of their way to vehemently argue their viewpoint. They're aggressive. They openly oppose and even ridicule belief.

➤ Rational Atheist—This group is also convinced that God doesn't exist and can be eager to debate and discuss the topic. However, rather than being angry and hostile, they prefer a calm and reasoned approach.

➤ Ornery Agnostic—Here, I'm borrowing some terminology from J. Edwin Orr, who said there are two kinds of agnostics: ornery ones and honest ones. Ornery ones say, "We don't know if there's a God because nobody *can* know." This makes me want to ask, "How do you know that? Is anyone really smart enough to be *sure* there's no God?"

➤ Honest Agnostic—Honest agnostics say, "I don't know for sure there's no God, but that doesn't mean I know that you don't know, and it doesn't mean that God doesn't exist. It only means that I haven't encountered Him in my personal experience and study to this point."

➤ Open Agnostic—This is someone who has not yet had a personal encounter with God but is open to the idea. In fact, those in this group are often willing to engage in conversations on the topic.

➤ Seeker—People in this category have a sense that there is more to God and faith than they have discovered so far. I've experienced seekers at different levels in their journey: some are mildly curious, others are open to discussion, still others are actively seeking, and some are literally trying to believe. (This last category includes the father who appealed to Jesus for healing for his son, and said, "I do believe; help me overcome my unbelief!" [Mark 9:24])

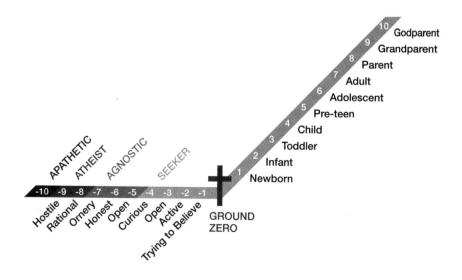

These general categories aren't intended to be derogatory in any way; they just help me determine what questions I might ask to help, and what needs others have that perhaps I can address. I want to be sensitive in responding to anyone in my life who might be responsive to God's life and love.

Peter challenges us to always be prepared to explain the hope we have in Christ to *everyone* who asks (1 Peter 3:15). I believe he's instructing us to always be ready to become spiritual parents, to help people find Christ, to allow God to use us to help someone else find Spirit life and reproduce in the Spirit.

I had a conversation with one man who appeared to be a difficult atheist—not exactly *hostile*, but quite self-assured and a bit intimidating. The two of us had an honest, open discussion. When he told me he was an atheist, I responded by asking, "What percentage of total knowledge do you believe you personally possess? Fifty percent? Thirty percent?"

He said he wasn't sure, so I continued, "I heard that Einstein claimed to understand five percent of total knowledge. Let me ask again: Of everything that can be known, what percent do you believe you know?"

This time, he responded, "Maybe two or three percent."

I explained, "Then isn't it reasonable that in the ninety-eight percent of knowable truth that you don't know, that God *could* exist?"

He replied, "Yes, that makes sense."

At that point, we agreed that he wasn't an atheist; he was an agnostic. It wasn't that he didn't believe God *could* exist, but that he personally didn't know it. I waded in again, "I've heard there are two kinds of agnostics, and I wonder which kind you are."

I explained the difference between ornery and honest, and he told me, "I think I'm an honest one. It isn't that I believe that God can't be known, but up to this point in my life, I don't know if there's a God."

I then explained that the way we get to know people is when they make themselves known to us, just like the way he and I were getting to know each other. And then I said that's what Jesus was doing for us, making God known so we could know Him as our heavenly Father. At that point, he abruptly said, "I don't want a father." It was clear to me that his pain was now talking. It was a family pain that many of us are more than familiar with. But we agreed together that there is a big difference between declaring, "There is no God" and saying "I don't want a father." I'm thankful for his intellectual honesty and that I was able to be a part of his journey from what he thought was intellectual atheism into a more tender region of honest relational truth. People are often open to such conversations. We need to be open in initiating them.

The recent global pandemic has made this an opportune time to initiate some of those conversations. Haven't you seen our culture's lifeless, Dead-Sea idols fail to provide the freshwater, life-giving, spiritual solutions we need? Some people worship sports and entertainment, but those outlets have been greatly restricted or shut down. Some people worship money and the economy, and many are now finding themselves on shaky financial ground. Some people worship government, politics, and the show of force, but as I write this we are in a pre-election turmoil rife with division and animosity. Some people worship science, and while I thank God for science and regularly pray for a vaccine, I don't worship it as God. People's idols are crumbling around them, and they are crying out, "Where is the life?" Only God can provide that answer for them, and He does that through us, through spiritual parenting.

Patience and Timing

Most parents know that their children, even the best of children, don't always respond to parental guidance. It's hard to convey meaningful truths if the child is eager to go be with friends, or his mind is someplace else, or she has just had a fight with a boyfriend. Wise parents wait for the right time to have serious, meaningful conversations. As a spiritual parent, the same may be true for you.

Some years ago, I was visiting an acquaintance in a Little Rock hospital. He and I had been involved in the same forum discussions on controversial topics at several private business luncheons. I was essentially the token pastor present, because most of the others were nonbelievers. The man I was visiting was a political businessman and leader in the community. He had enjoyed ridiculing me for my faith on several occasions, but that day he had been told his case was terminal and he would not be returning home.

I had the opportunity to share my story and explain how Jesus' death and resurrection provide eternal life, joy, and hope to all who believe. That day there was no ridicule from him. From his deathbed, point blank, he asked me, "How can I know I'm going to heaven?" I told him that Jesus said whoever denies Him before men, He would deny before His Father in heaven. But whoever confesses Him before men, He would also confess before His Father (Matthew 10:32-33). My friend blurted right out, "I confess Him! I confess Him!"

I'll never forget that. As we prayed, he asked Christ to come into his life, to forgive his sins, and to give him eternal life. And I was privileged to tell that story at his memorial service only days later. Do you know what happened? His Dead-Sea life was made vibrantly alive in God's cleansing fresh water.

In Ezekiel's vision, he saw the Arabah, the geological depression where the Dead Sea lies. It was there, at the lowest place on the planet, with water so salty that nothing can live, where the Lord was going to infuse a river of fresh water until it was teeming with life. What's the message? Nobody's too far from God if we are willing to channel His life there. Just as God can make the Dead Sea spring to life, He can resurrect spiritually dead people who haven't yet received His wonderful life . . . and He can use you in that way.

I learned a song in the early stages of my spiritual discipleship that reminds me of this passage in Ezekiel:

> I've got a river of life flowing out of me
> Makes the lame to walk and the blind to see
> Opens prison doors, sets the captives free.
> I've got a river of life flowing out of me.[20]

This is God's song for every believer. As we continue to mature and grow into His fullness, He wants that river of life to become a spillway, offering a fresh life to a dead world. When we let God's river flow and share the good news of Christ with others, God takes us to the level of a spiritual parent. You can let God's light shine through to you to bring the joy of life to another. Are you a spiritual parent yet? This is what God designs for you. That's what He wants you to be.

So, what are your next steps today? Start with prayer. Think through how you came to know the Lord, and jot it down. How did you realize your need? What prayer did you pray as you turned to God to follow Christ? What changes have you experienced since choosing to receive Christ?

Pray in the Spirit and ask God to lead you. Then give yourself permission to follow His prompting and do whatever He places on your mind to do. Be willing to share your story and trust God with the results. You may run into some resistance and obstacles along the way, but push through them. If your palms get sweaty, dry them off and keep going. Keep growing!

If you wait until you think you're ready to do it, it's probably not going to happen.

I've been told that the most transformative experience a biological adult can have is becoming a parent, and I hear lots of parents say, "If you wait until you think you're ready to have a child, you'll never have one." I believe the same is true about sharing the gospel. If you wait until you think you're ready to do it, it's probably not going to happen. But I've found that you learn how to do it by doing it. You step in, and the spiritual growth that results is, beyond doubt, transformative. It brings life not just to the recipient of the good news, but to the bearer of that good news as well. May God's life-giving water flow in and through you today. And may you feel the smile of God as you become a spillway of His life into our world in such great need.

STAGE	LESSON
Godparent	♪
Grandparent	
Parent	Allow God to change the world by changing you. Become willing to take his life-giving water to others' Dead-Sea lives.
Adult	Take responsibility for your own spiritual life. Be filled to the whole measure of the fullness of Christ.
Adolescent	Develop. Suit up in spiritual armor, step into your spiritual warrior, and join the battle.
Preteen	Discover who you are: your identity in Christ, where you belong, and your destiny in fulfilling God's will.
Child	Put knowledge into action. Obey God in active faith.
Toddler	Learn to walk in faith and talk to God in prayer as you grow in community with God and others.
Infant	Receive nourishing care from your loving heavenly Father and other spiritual "parents" who want to help you grow.
Newborn	Be born again and receive God's wonderful new life.

ADVENTURE PAGES

Pilot's Flight Plan

1. What experiences have you had so far, if any, with spiritual parenting? What were the results? Have you missed any opportunities due to fear or not knowing how to proceed?

2. What would you say is your current level of spiritual maturity and involvement with the flow of God's water/Spirit in your life? Are you ankle deep, knee deep, waist deep, or fully immersed? Do you think you're ready to go deeper? Explain your answer.

3. Have you had any challenging or difficult conversations with atheists or agnostics? What might you do or say differently next time?

4. How have you seen people respond to all the uncertainty of life today as their various "idols" have crumbled in the wake of the pandemic? Do you see opportunity to initiate conversations of life and hope during these times?

5. How can you see God changing the world by changing you?

Course Correction

If you only do one thing, do this: On your phone, your bathroom mirror, your computer, or whatever you see regularly, write down the names of the three people you've thought about as you read this chapter.

Captain's Log

If you're helping a spiritual parent grow, I suggest:

➤ Discuss the continuum from unbelief to faith in Christ, identify the place of each name on the person's list, and craft a connection plan.

➤ Pray with him or her for the three people on the list.

➤ Share some tools or communication strategies that have helped you make the gospel clear to people in your life.

BECOMING LOLLI & POPS

GRANDPARENT

"There is no success without a successor."

—Peter Drucker

I became a grandfather reluctantly. I didn't know what to expect, but I remember thinking, *I'm not ready to have grandkids. That's something old people do. I still have mountains to move and dragons to slay. I'm not done with life yet.*

To be truthful, I hadn't given the matter much thought, and when I finally did, I didn't much care for the results. I don't know what comes to your mind when you hear the word *grandparent*, but for me, that meant aging, wrinkling, and long hours in rocking chairs. It meant I'd probably begin to emit that unusually distinctive smell I'd always associated with *my* grandparents. Was it now my turn to drift along and fade into the sunset as the rest of the world kept whizzing by?

Regardless, I eventually discovered that I didn't have much of a say in the matter. I didn't get a vote. The day came when I was told, "You're a grandfather!" And now that I've been through that experience more than once, I think I'm qualified to speak with authority. If and when that day ever arrives for you, I have six words of advice: *Come on in, the water's fine.*

I didn't see it coming. Something happened that I can't explain. I got blindsided by a whole new level of joy. I was smitten. I was immediately in love—and now it's happened twice! My new hobby is doting—showing up with gifts and making sure West and Cedar get two desserts if they want them. My wife Lisa is Lolli and I'm Pops. Clearly, we went for the cheesiest names we could find, and I'm fine with that! West couldn't pronounce L's for a while, so we were temporarily Woly & Pops.

Anyway, if you're having any fears and trepidations about becoming a grandparent, don't. Come on in. The water's fine. I know our culture idolizes youth and that something in every one of us says, "I don't want to get old." I realize adulting is chaotic, complicated, and full of challenge, conflict, and ambiguity. But it's also one of those things that you can only learn by doing—like learning how to swim. You don't learn how to swim by reading a book, attending a webinar, or watching a YouTube video. Those things might help prepare you, but if you want to learn to swim, you have to get in the water.

Spiritual Grandparents

The same is true for *spiritual* adulting at all levels. We've already determined that God's design isn't for you to finally become a spiritually mature adult and then stop growing. No, there's more growing to be done, but at these upper stages, you'll need to be more intentional than ever about your spiritual growth. It's easy to "sit out" a lot of opportunities that come your way. You can only continue to grow when you choose to keep expanding your influence and take your leadership to the next level. Now we're talking about spiritual grandparenting.

Becoming a spiritual grandparent isn't about losing touch with work, with the world, or with life. It's a spiritual age of engaging and impacting, generating life and leadership in others. It's the stage of life for what the apostle John calls the *fathers* of spiritual growth (1 John 2:13). It's the stage for spiritual elders, for sages in life.

Lisa and I are thrilled every time we're with our grandsons, West and Cedar, partially because they enable us to see life through their eyes and be a child all over again. But that's not the main reason. Neither do we attempt to hijack their lives and live vicariously through them. (I've seen that happen, and it's not a good thing.) What I enjoy most about grandparenthood is envisioning and enriching my grandchildren's own uniqueness for an even greater impact and influence in the world to come. It's a world I will not be a part of, except through my investment in them.

Isaac Newton said: "If I have seen further it is by standing on the shoulders of Giants." Spiritual grandparenting is lending your shoulders to those who are yet to rise. It means increasing the impact of your life by investing in those who can see farther than you will because of your influence on them. It's what Paul tells Timothy to do: "The things you have heard me say in the presence of many witnesses entrust to reliable people who will also be qualified to teach others" (2 Timothy 2:2). Count 'em. That short sentence covers multiple levels of cascading influence: Paul, to Timothy, to "many witnesses," to "reliable people," and to "others." Paul is advocating the practices of mentoring and modeling that will multiply ministry forward. That's the opportunity and responsibility of spiritual grandparents, and it has very little to do with biological age.

From Addition to Multiplication

We see a similar cascade of influence in the early church detailed in the book of Acts. The book begins with the ascension of Jesus into heaven (Acts 1:1-11), the coming of the Holy Spirit (Acts 2:1-13), and the rapid growth of the church. The number of believers at Jesus' ascension was a meager 120 (Acts 1:15), but after Peter's impassioned sermon on the Day of Pentecost, another three thousand believers were added (Acts 2:41). From that point, we are told, "the Lord added to their number daily those who were being saved" (Acts 2:47). As ministry and growth continued, the same word for "added" is used again a short time later: "More and more men and women believed in the Lord and were added to their number" (Acts 5:14).

But before long, the language changed: "And the word of God increased; and the number of the disciples *multiplied* in Jerusalem greatly" (Acts 6:7 KJV, emphasis added). The increasing numbers have stopped being added and have started multiplying. Why? What changed? If we look at the opening verses of Acts 6, we discover that Jesus' apostles, the church leaders, had just designated seven men (maturing believers who were not apostles) and had prayed over them to become ministry mentors for others. The apostles took the grandparent role, empowered the next generation, and initiated a process that ramped up the already healthy growth of the church. The process was:

Evangelize ➜ *Disciple* ➜ *Mentor* ➜ *Multiply.*

At the time, the Roman Empire was saturated with false gods, and polytheism was practiced everywhere. Sensuality and sexuality were woven into their religious rites. Five million slaves were central to an oppressive social system that dominated women and children. Powerful Roman legions fueled a military that conquered nations and destroyed anybody that got in their way.

This was the world where 120 followers of Jesus started a movement. It was in this world where the apostles went out to evangelize, to disciple, and to mentor . . . and taught others in the church to do the same. This process proved so effective that it reached a tipping point and changed the entire culture. Who would have imagined the efforts of that small and persecuted sect would Christianize the entire Roman world? Yet by a.d. 323, Christianity became the official religion of the Empire.

The rapid growth of the early church was due to believers who were growing into their God-given potentials, moving through the spiritual stages we have been examining, from childhood into adolescence, and on into spiritual adulthood. They were becoming spiritual parents who could share salvation and offer God's life to others. But the church really began to flourish when a few spiritual grandparents began to mentor another faithful generation and multiply their influence and their impact to the Roman world. This was God's design . . . and it still is.

The good news for all of us is that growing into a spiritual grandparent is not a matter of chronological age; it's a matter of impact. Some people get far along in calendar years and never mature spiritually. Don't let that happen to you. Instead, regardless of your age, you can begin to multiply influence as the ones you help to find life in Christ begin to lead others to Christ as well. That's what success is.

Business management expert Peter Drucker observed, "There is no success without a successor."[21] The power of spiritual grandparenting comes from breeding success in Christ beyond yourself, through those whom you disciple and mentor, creating an ongoing cascade of influence that results in multiplication rather than addition of new believers.

Logically, of course, you can't become a grandparent before you become a parent, but in fact, Jesus became both on the same day!

Jesus, the Spiritual Parent

Did you know that Jesus became a spiritual grandparent in his early 30s? Logically, of course, you can't become a grandparent before you become a parent, but in fact, Jesus became both on the same day! It happened in the most unlikely place with the most unlikely person that anyone could have imagined. You may know the story.

Now [Jesus] had to go through Samaria. So he came to a town in Samaria called Sychar, near the plot of ground Jacob had given to his son Joseph. Jacob's well was there, and Jesus, tired as he was from the journey, sat down by the well. It was about noon.

When a Samaritan woman came to draw water, Jesus said to her, "Will you give me a drink?" (His disciples had gone into the town to buy food.)

The Samaritan woman said to him, "You are a Jew and I am a Samaritan woman. How can you ask me for a drink?" (For Jews do not associate with Samaritans.)

Jesus answered her, "If you knew the gift of God and who it is that asks you for a drink, you would have asked him and he would have given you living water."

"Sir," the woman said, "you have nothing to draw with and the well is deep. Where can you get this living water? Are you greater than our father Jacob, who gave us the well and drank from it himself, as did also his sons and his livestock?"

Jesus answered, "Everyone who drinks this water will be thirsty again, but whoever drinks the water I give them will never thirst. Indeed, the water I give them will become in them a spring of water welling up to eternal life."

The woman said to him, "Sir, give me this water so that I won't get thirsty and have to keep coming here to draw water."

He told her, "Go, call your husband and come back."

"I have no husband," she replied.

Jesus said to her, "You are right when you say you have no husband. The fact is, you have had five husbands, and the man you now have is not your husband. What you have just said is quite true."

"Sir," the woman said, "I can see that you are a prophet. Our ancestors worshiped on this mountain, but you Jews claim that the place where we must worship is in Jerusalem."

"Woman," Jesus replied, "believe me, a time is coming when you will worship the Father neither on this mountain nor in Jerusalem. You Samaritans worship what you do not know; we worship what we do know, for salvation is from the Jews. Yet a time is coming and has now come when the true worshipers will worship the Father in the Spirit and in truth, for they are the kind of worshipers the Father seeks. God is spirit, and his worshipers must worship in the Spirit and in truth."

The woman said, "I know that Messiah" (called Christ) "is coming. When he comes, he will explain everything to us."

Then Jesus declared, "I, the one speaking to you—I am he." (John 4:1-26)

This account is filled with fascinating little tidbits. To begin with, Jesus is alone at a well. Why? Because it apparently took twelve men to gather enough food for a group of thirteen. But the disciples' absence allowed for a private and sensitive conversation to take place.

Then, when a woman comes out to get water at high noon, the hottest part of the day, she's by herself. What's up with that? Women typically gathered water in the cool of the day, either early or late, and it was usually a group activity—a time for socializing and chatting it up. But not her. Why?

We eventually get some answers during the conversation that Jesus strikes up with her. Jesus is tired and thirsty, so He asks her for a drink . . . which shocks her on two levels. First, He's a Jew and she's a Samaritan. Different ethnic groups. Second, He's a man and she's a woman. In that culture, respectable men didn't connect in any way with unknown women. The conversation becomes even more scandalous when we see that Jesus knew exactly what kind of woman she was, yet He continued their discussion and guided it to the point of offering her living water. We examined that symbol for salvation in the previous chapter.

Read through the account again, and this time notice how Jesus keeps the focus on what's most important throughout the conversation. Every one of us, when we're trying to engage with another person, will sometimes encounter certain barriers to belief. Jesus did, and He modeled for us how to deal with them. He wanted this woman to come to know salvation through Him as Messiah, so He took on the spiritual parent role to help her find new birth into Spirit life. But let's take a closer look at the obstacles, or walls, that might have short-circuited her ability to receive spiritual life.

The wall of location

The woman was in Samaria, which was the wrong side of the tracks for respectable Jews of the first century. When traveling, most Jewish people would go well out of their way to avoid an itinerary through Samaria, but Jesus didn't. He could have taken a roundabout route, but the text says He *had* to go through Samaria. Jesus didn't tear down the wall; He just acknowledged it and went around it.

The wall of self-concern

Jesus was finally away from all the crowds with some time to himself. Even His disciples were gone, providing a rare period of peace and quiet. Besides, He was hot, tired, and ready for some R&R. When the woman approached, most other people would probably think, *You know, I really need some ME time.* And if Jesus had ignored the woman, she would likely have gone about her business and left without saying a word. In fact, that was the expected social protocol. Yet instead of staying behind that wall, Jesus moved around it and asked, "Will you give me a drink?"

The wall of sexism

In response to Jesus' question, the woman immediately erected a wall. She countered with the gender barrier, and gender bias in their culture was deep, thick, and strong. Jesus didn't let it stop Him. He just went around it.

The wall of racism

Before Jesus could even respond, the woman doubled down with the issue of prejudice: "You are a Jew and I am a Samaritan woman." She was bringing up a longstanding sensitive issue. She, a Samaritan, was part of the mixed racial group descended from Jewish people left behind after the Babylonians and Assyrians had conquered Israel and taken the best and brightest of their people and material goods. In time, the Jewish survivors left behind had intermarried with non-Jews, eventually creating the Samaritan people. Over the centuries, the disdain and outright hatred of Samaritans by Jews had only intensified. But Jesus didn't get sidetracked. He made no effort to deny the problem of prejudice. Instead, He simply went around the wall and kept the conversation going.

The wall of moralism

As the dialog continues, we find a clue for why the Samaritan woman would be out in the heat of the day by herself: multiple men in her life. She's had five husbands and was living with yet another man. This was a past she wanted to keep to herself, but Jesus let her know, with no judgment attached, that He knew all about it. It makes me wonder: Was she known as a homewrecker back in town? Is that why she was out there all by herself? And yet Jesus doesn't let her reputation stop Him. He speaks to it and then keeps the conversation going.

The wall of religion

Probably eager to steer the conversation away from her private life, the woman brought up doctrine and worship style. Unwelcome at the temple in Jerusalem, the Samaritans gathered on a different mountain to worship. Although still steeped in Judaism, they had veered away from some of the basics, which Jesus pointed out. Yet the woman was spiritually attuned enough to realize that she was talking to someone with spiritual insight, someone worthy of respect.

The wall of politics

You can argue that the woman broaches a barrier of politics when she says, "You Jews claim that the place where we must worship is in Jerusalem." Our culture is not the first to interweave religion and politics. The temple in Jerusalem was much more than a church; it was a center of all aspects of Jewish life—the spiritual and political center of the nation. So the woman was hitting a hot button and saying, essentially, "We Samaritans are on the total opposite side of the aisle from you Jews." Jesus doesn't let her political comment hijack the conversation. He responds and keeps sharing His truth.

How does Jesus respond? He doesn't take the bait. He navigates every obstacle, moves around every wall, and instead lets each potential barrier become a bridge to further discussion.

The Samaritan woman, though fascinated with Jesus and His wisdom, seems to do everything she can to derail this conversation. How does Jesus respond? He doesn't take the bait. He navigates every obstacle, moves around every wall, and instead lets each potential barrier become a bridge to further discussion. Throughout their talk, He shows himself full of grace and truth, and finally introduces himself to her as the Messiah she had been waiting for.

Helpful Tips from A to . . . G

This story gives us a model of how we can become better spiritual mentors. By following Jesus' example, we become spiritual parents who help others find Christ.

And no, I haven't forgotten, I'm going to show you how Jesus became a spiritual grandfather in His early thirties. But first I want to show you what we all can learn from His model of spiritual mentoring.

I first learned the following concepts from a book by Paul Little. I have since used an alphabetical device to help me remember them. I hope it will help you, too, as you apply the ABC's of making friends for God.

Associate with non-Christians.

Jesus could easily have avoided any contact with the woman at the well, yet He not only ventured into Samaria, He then superseded the boundaries of race, gender, social convention, religion, and politics to engage in a conversation through which He could share His spiritual life with this woman. People who make friends for God are not self-righteous snobs who keep their distance. They are warm-hearted human beings who connect with others who may be quite unlike us. If you want to catch fish, you go where the fish are, right? That's what Jesus is doing here.

Build bridges.

In asking for a drink, Jesus established a common point of interest and at the same time acknowledged the woman as someone who could meet a need that He had. His was a startling request, because no self-respecting Jew at the time would ever use the same dish as a Samaritan. But to help the woman find the truth she was seeking, Jesus offered himself as a bridge builder. To make friends for God, we too must be bridge builders and look for common points of interest.

Just recently, one of my friends told me he uses five H's to build bridges and start spiritual conversations with others:

1. Share your personal Histories with one another.

2. Ask about the person's Heroes. Who does he or she admire, and why?

3. What are the Highlights of the person's life—the events that stand out?

4. What are the person's Heartaches? (You're now getting into more tender space.)

5. Finally, where does he or she find Hope?

Remember that this is a conversation, not an interview. Don't dominate the discussion, and don't let the other person do all the talking. As you move through the H's and the other person shares, share your story and ideas, too. One of the questions that I sometimes ask people who have not yet expressed faith in Christ is: "Do you ever think about spiritual things?" That allows me to honestly say, "For a while I never did, but then something happened that turned the corner for me." It has been a really natural way for me to start a spiritual conversation with people I don't know.

Create interest.

Jesus first kindled the woman's curiosity by talking to her in public. He showed a genuine interest in someone who expected to be overlooked. And He didn't just nod hello; He gradually took the conversation to a deeper level and kept her attention and involvement. These days, just being sincerely interested in another person can arouse curiosity. In fact, others may be suspicious at first, but they'll probably respond when they see you're sincere.

A good sense of humor is also a plus to help create interest. Paul Little said, "Contrary to popular belief, Christians don't have to give up their sense of humor when they become Christians. . . . We may not indulge in the same kind of humor as others, but we can be spontaneous and find laughter and zest in everyday life. Moreover, we know there is wholesome humor and delight in living every day for Jesus Christ."[22]

Like Jesus, we ought to offer a relationship, not force a message. Be ready to share how Christ relates to your everyday life and then gives you more peace of mind, purpose, meaning, and strength to face the challenges that we all have.

Don't go too far, too fast.

Jesus was sensitive as He spoke to the woman's needs, and sensitivity can't be rushed. Likewise, we need to regularly assess how much other people are ready to hear and deal with, and then share in a gentle way they can easily respond to.

Express understanding.

When Jesus brought up the marital status of the woman at the well and let her know He was aware of her long series of husbands, He wasn't accusatory but rather spoke matter-of-factly. He didn't condemn her previous indiscretions, but He didn't condone them either. By not making her feel embarrassed or uncomfortable, He helped her gracefully confront her past in light of His grace and truth.

We should expect people to be sinners with messy lives, and we should meet them where they are. It's not our job to tell them how bad they are, but rather to share God's love with them, show them how much He cares, and describe the difference He can make.

Follow through.

When the woman tried to hide behind the walls of religious procedure and social/political differences, Jesus steered the conversation back to personal relationship with God and how God is bigger than those differences. To Jesus (and to us), "The main thing is to keep the main thing the main thing" in a nonthreatening way. We should also be ready for excuses that come our way and controversial topics that might arise. We can assure people that God is bigger than the messes we find ourselves in. We can know Him personally, through Jesus Christ, and we can worship Him in Spirit and truth.

Give them Christ.

John Wesley, the great Methodist evangelist, said, "I go into a town and I give them Christ." That's the whole heart and message of the good news. As Christ-followers going out into a world in need, our task is not to share a new set of rules, a philosophy of life, or a political platform. It's not even about going to church or becoming increasingly religious—not at first, anyway. Rather, our goal is to introduce others into a loving relationship with a living Christ and then invite them to get to know Him. That's the starting point, the foundation for everything else.

Jesus, the Spiritual Grandparent

Now, you might be wondering: "Isn't this just a rehash of being a spiritual parent that you already covered in the last chapter?" Well, yes. Helping people meet Christ is the role of spiritual parents, but it's also the necessary first step toward becoming a spiritual grandparent. You can't become a spiritual grandparent until you've helped somebody come to Jesus.

You can't become a spiritual grandparent until you've helped somebody come to Jesus.

And let me guess your next question: "Didn't you say the account of the woman at the well is a story about Jesus becoming a spiritual grandparent?" Absolutely. Check out the rest of the story:

> Then, leaving her water jar, the woman went back to the town and said to the people, "Come, see a man who told me everything I ever did. Could this be the Messiah?" They came out of the town and made their way toward him. . . .

Many of the Samaritans from that town believed in him because of the woman's testimony, "He told me everything I ever did." So when the Samaritans came to him, they urged him to stay with them, and he stayed two days. And because of his words many more became believers.

They said to the woman, "We no longer believe just because of what you said; now we have heard for ourselves, and we know that this man really is the Savior of the world." (John 4:28-30; 39-42)

The woman left behind her water jar, perhaps because she'd had a taste of living water flowing into her Dead-Sea life like Ezekiel described in the previous chapter. She went back into town, started telling everyone who would listen about Jesus and what just happened to her, and they believed because of her testimony. Barely a spiritual newborn, she immediately became a spiritual parent by helping many others come to Christ. And at the same moment, Jesus became a spiritual grandparent with a town full of spiritual grandbabies.

That's how you become a spiritual grandparent, too. That's how new generations can come to Christ. Cities, nations, and empires can come to Christ. As you tell your story, and others join God's story, God's life comes alive and continues to flow full and free. God's kingdom flourishes and God's will is done on earth as it is in heaven. You'll shift from *adding* to the kingdom, to seeing the kingdom *multiply*.

And I hope your story ends the way this one did, with many new believers doing everything they can to discover for themselves more about the love and forgiveness of Christ. Our world is filled with people who still need to hear. May we become the spiritual parents and grandparents who will help them arrive at life-changing and eternal truth.

Come on in. The water's fine.

STAGE	LESSON
Godparent	
Grandparent	Move from adding to God's kingdom to multiplying the kingdom by mentoring your spiritual children to share the gospel.
Parent	Allow God to change the world by changing you. Become willing to take his life-giving water to others' Dead-Sea lives.
Adult	Take responsibility for your own spiritual life. Be filled to the whole measure of the fullness of Christ.
Adolescent	Develop. Suit up in spiritual armor, step into your spiritual warrior, and join the battle.
Preteen	Discover who you are: your identity in Christ, where you belong, and your destiny in fulfilling God's will.
Child	Put knowledge into action. Obey God in active faith.
Toddler	Learn to walk in faith and talk to God in prayer as you grow in community with God and others.
Infant	Receive nourishing care from your loving heavenly Father and other spiritual "parents" who want to help you grow.
Newborn	Be born again and receive God's wonderful new life.

ADVENTURE PAGES

Pilot's Flight Plan

1. Think about Isaac Newton's statement: "If I have seen further it is by standing on the shoulders of Giants." Who are some "giants" who contributed to your ability to see Jesus Christ more clearly? In what ways are you passing along what you've learned from them to the next generations?

2. The process used by the early church to expand the awareness and influence of God's kingdom was:

   Evangelize ➔ *Disciple* ➔ *Mentor* ➔ *Multiply.*

   Which of these steps do you do best? As a spiritual grandparent, where might you need to devote more attention?

3. What are some "walls" you've encountered as you've attempted to talk to others about Jesus? Were you able to get around them?

4. Which of the A-to-G suggestions for sharing your faith was most beneficial as you consider how you might connect better with other people?

5. What were some of your insights and takeaways after seeing how Jesus interacted with the woman at the well?

Course Correction

If you only do one thing, do this: Talk to your pastor or mentor to come up with a plan to equip the people you lead to share their faith.

Captain's Log

If you're helping a spiritual grandparent grow, I suggest:

➤ The person has, by now, become a peer, so listen as much as you teach.

➤ Share tools, podcasts, training material, and other resources to help the person equip others to communicate the Good News about Jesus.

➤ Take the person along with you to share the gospel with someone.

A BRIDGE TO LIFE

GODPARENT

> "We are all worms, but I do believe that
> I am a glow worm."
>
> **—Winston Churchill**

The Choluteca bridge stands strong and sturdy in the city of Choluteca, Honduras. It just doesn't stand over the Choluteca River.

The original Choluteca bridge was built in the 1930s by the U.S. Army Corps of Engineers and is a famous work of architecture. However, Honduras is subject to regular hurricanes, many quite severe, which often requires bridges to be repaired or replaced. So in the 1990s, the government commissioned a Japanese company to build a new bridge using the latest technology—one that was said to be hurricane-proof.

The new Choluteca bridge was completed in 1998, and only months later Hurricane Mitch arrived in its full category-five fury. The second-deadliest Atlantic hurricane by that time, it caused seven thousand deaths in Honduras. Many Honduran bridges were destroyed, and many others, including the old Choluteca bridge, were damaged. Of course, everyone wanted to know how their new bridge had fared. It was essentially unscathed.

However (and this is a big *however*), while the power of the hurricane hadn't affected the bridge, it had completely rerouted the course of the Choluteca River. Ever since the hurricane, the river now flows *beside* the new Choluteca bridge—not *under* it. Additionally, the roads to the bridge were washed away, and the expensive new structure was immediately labeled "the bridge to nowhere."

You can look up current photos of this bridge spanning dry ground beside the river. I have one right across from my desk in my office so I never forget this testament to the engineering genius and limited foresight of humanity. I see this immovable bridge to nowhere as a heads-up for the church.

Bridges and Ladders

The Latin word for priest is *pontifex*. It means "bridge builder" or "bridge maker." The term applies to all believers, because the role of God's people includes being a *kingdom of priests*. Peter reminds us: "You are a chosen people, a royal priesthood, a holy nation" (1 Peter 2:9). As priests, we're bridge makers: people through whom God intends to extend connections into our broken and needy world.

God often chooses to act in this world through obedient human beings. People like you and me align our lives to His will so that it can be done on earth as it is in heaven. What I try to remember as I look at my photo of the Choluteca bridge is that attempting to build an institutional church that will withstand every storm of life may be wasted effort. Jesus Christ is the solid, immovable rock on which the church is built, yet the church—the people of God—need not be fixed and rigid. It's more important that we stay nimble, adaptive, and relevant.

The church must be nimble; the church must be adaptive. The church must be able to ride the waves and changes of culture, yet stay on mission to a world in need. We need to be bridge builders, but we don't need any more bridges to nowhere. We have a better option.

During World War II, especially in the European theater, the United States used pontoon bridges, which were portable prefab modular units that could span rivers. Pontoons could support troops and even carry tanks into enemy territory. They were portable bridges that could float into any gap. Since they were not stationary, pontoon bridges could move to wherever people needed them.

Believers aren't just supposed to be bridges to connect people with the love and grace of Jesus; we're supposed to be *the right kind* of bridges.

Believers aren't just supposed to be bridges to connect people with the love and grace of Jesus; we're supposed to be *the right kind* of bridges. You can be hard, strong, and unshakeable . . . and still be a bridge to nowhere if you don't reflect the compassion of Christ. When we choose that course, we make ourselves irrelevant and immediately obsolete. Far better is to be a pontoon—to be ready to go wherever the need is, always flexible and supportive. When Jesus builds His church, His focus is building the people in whom He lives and through whom He makes himself known in this world (Matthew 16:18-20).

This book has been about spiritual growth—growth in becoming the bridges of life God intends. We've created a chart to track our coming to faith and new birth in Christ, up through spiritual childhood, into our adolescence, to the final stages of spiritual adulthood. As we complete our chart in this chapter, you'll notice that it represents a ladder. The first seven stages are the lower rungs that refer to your individual personal growth, as you climb ever higher. In those stages you remain focused on your own spiritual progress. Then, as a spiritual adult, the way you keep climbing is to become a spiritual parent. You share your story of how salvation made a difference for you, and you help others come alive in Christ and start up the ladder for themselves. Then, as the ones you led to Christ begin to help others find Him, you reach the next level of spiritual grandparent where you see generations of spiritual life being reproduced and many people coming to know Jesus as Savior and Lord.

That's the image of the ladder. It's the path to Christ. After you find it, you help others find it. And after they find it, they help still others find it. Eventually, you can see people coming from all around as you and other generations are helping even more people find the ladder.

In this chapter we come to the final rung, the highest level: Spiritual Godparent. A social godparent in a family culture is someone specially designated when a child is still very young to commit to that child's spiritual upbringing. In many cases, the godparent becomes a mentor to assist the parents in providing training to help the child develop a personal relationship with Jesus Christ. Or if for some reason the parents become unable or unwilling to attend to the child's spiritual growth, that role falls to the godparent.

STAGE	LESSON
Godparent	Everywhere you go, be a bridge that connects other people with God. When people look at you, they see Christ.
Grandparent	Move from adding to God's kingdom to multiplying the kingdom by mentoring your spiritual children to share the gospel.
Parent	Allow God to change the world by changing you. Become willing to take his life-giving water to others' Dead-Sea lives.

Adult	Take responsibility for your own spiritual life. Be filled to the whole measure of the fullness of Christ.
Adolescent	Develop. Suit up in spiritual armor, step into your spiritual warrior, and join the battle.
Preteen	Discover who you are: your identity in Christ, where you belong, and your destiny in fulfilling God's will.
Child	Put knowledge into action. Obey God in active faith.
Toddler	Learn to walk in faith and talk to God in prayer as you grow in community with God and others.
Infant	Receive nourishing care from your loving heavenly Father and other spiritual "parents" who want to help you grow.
Newborn	Be born again and receive God's wonderful new life.

So . . . what is a *spiritual godparent*? At this final stage of spiritual growth, you don't just move up the ladder for yourself like you did as an adult. You don't just help someone else find it, like a spiritual parent. You even go beyond mentoring and multiplying influence like a spiritual grandparent. What's the telltale sign that you are now living as a spiritual godparent? *You take the ladder with you, everywhere you go.* Your life extends the ladder to every person you meet. You're ready to share not just your story, but Christ's story.

As I said in the Introduction of this book, salvation isn't simply a ticket to heaven when you die. It's not merely a fire insurance policy to escape hell. Rather, salvation is a growing opportunity in relationship and resource to face every challenge of life in Christ. Paul's prayer for the

Ephesian church has been mentioned in previous chapters, but it bears repeating here. It's an appropriate challenge for all of us as we arrive at this final stage of spiritual growth:

> I pray that you, being rooted and established in love, may have power, together with all the Lord's holy people, to grasp how wide and long and high and deep is the love of Christ, and to know this love that surpasses knowledge—that you may be filled to the measure of all the fullness of God. (Ephesians 3:17-20)

Even your wounds and broken places become God's opportunity to bring healing and strength.

Filled to the measure of all the fullness of God. This is an incredible expectation. Your life becomes sacred space where God increases your capacity to know Him and make Him known in deeper, higher, richer ways. Even your wounds and broken places become God's opportunity to bring healing and strength. In the same way that a Japanese kintsugi artisan repairs broken places in pottery by filling the cracks with gold, God pours His priceless Spirit into our souls, filling our brokenness with more of His fullness. As He fills your life, it changes you—and your life, as a sacred space, grows larger. That's what this book has been about—increasing your capacity to reveal more and more of who God is to the world—to reflect more of God's righteous character, to demonstrate more of God's justice and peace, to bear the fruit of His Spirit and the gifts of His Spirit, and to live a life full of grace and truth, as Christ did. This is the fulfillment of Jesus' promise: "I chose you and appointed you so that you might go and bear fruit, fruit that will last" (John 15:16). He assures us, "This is to my Father's glory that you bear much fruit, showing yourselves to be my disciples" (John 15:8).

Deeper Water

We saw this advanced level of spiritual maturity foreshadowed back in Chapter 8 as we examined the vision of Ezekiel 47, with the river of life flowing from the temple. As Ezekiel walked into the river, he didn't stop when it got ankle deep, knee deep, or even waist deep. He made a point of noting that the river was deep enough to swim in. What do you suppose he meant by that?

Here's how I like to look at it: when you watch a swimmer in a river, what do you see? You see the person's head. Right? They're putting their whole body into swimming, but it is the head that remains prominent. Now, who is the head of the church? Jesus Christ. The church is His body; He's the head. When you tell God you want Him to make your life His sacred space, and then He fills you to "the measure of all His fullness," doesn't it make sense that others then start seeing Christ in you? People look at you, a member of the body of Christ, but they see the head: Christ's love, God's wisdom, and Spirit life coming through you. You begin to add divine value wherever you go.

That's being a spiritual godparent. At this level, you're "all in" for God. You're in the deep water. Even better, you're now a living bridge where people can connect with God. Instead of bringing others to the bridge to find security in the storm, you *become* the bridge. Wherever you go, you're an opportunity for people to access God through you. The institutional church isn't the bridge to life; God's people are. The bridge isn't just where the church building is; a connection to God is made wherever His people go. That's what it means to be "a chosen people, a royal priesthood, a holy nation" (1 Peter 2:9). It's God's people acting as Christ's ambassadors: "as though God were making his appeal through us" (2 Corinthians 5:20).

It's the powerful result of sharing our story—and Christ's story—with others. That's part of what it means to be in the priesthood of believers.

I'm reminded of the last verse of that old song, "Have Thine Own Way, Lord." What a great prayer:

> Have Thine own way, Lord, have Thine own way;
> Hold o'er my being absolute sway.
> Fill with Thy Spirit till all shall see
> Christ only, always, living in me.[23]

It takes a very mature-ish believer to pray, "What You want for me, Lord, is what I want for me. Nothing more. Nothing less. Nothing else." This is this attitude of a spiritual godparent.

It's also the attitude of Christ himself who prayed, in the Garden of Gethsemane, "Father, if you are willing, take this cup from me; yet not my will, but yours be done" (Luke 22:42). Of course, you know what happened next, right? Jesus endured the worst of sin and death that the spiritual enemy could unleash on Him, but God transformed that horrible experience into the best thing that could ever happen. God turned a crucifixion into a resurrection. As a result, the world now has the opportunity to find salvation, God's living water, and eternal life.

Unexpected Godparents

Jesus wasn't the first to pray that prayer, however. Two other people very close to Him shared that desire to place God's will above their own. Both were experiencing levels of brokenness at the time, and both could rightfully be called godparents, although not exactly in the traditional sense that we use the term today. One was Mary, the other was Joseph.

God had a powerful plan in mind for the lives of Mary and Joseph: they would be invited to parent God. Whoa! That made them the first godparents, and indeed, the only ones to literally be God's parents. But before they could fully commit to aligning themselves to God's will, they both went through separate crucibles of surrender.

Mary is believed to be quite a young woman when an angel appeared to her with startling news: "Do not be afraid, Mary; you have found favor with God. You will conceive and give birth to a son, and you are to call him Jesus. He will be great and will be called the Son of the Most High. The Lord God will give him the throne of his father David, and he will reign over Jacob's descendants forever; his kingdom will never end" (Luke 1:30-33). Mary had no idea how she, a virgin, could have a child, but the angel assured her that God would make it happen.

Mary's response reflected great faith: "I am the Lord's servant. May your word to me be fulfilled" (Luke 1:38). Was there a broken human heart in that prayer? What Mary was really saying was, "Lord, what You want for me is what I want for me, even if it means leaving Joseph behind." She was engaged and looking ahead to a normal married life. Humanly speaking, she knew this would change everything. To say "Yes" to God meant surrendering her dreams, including her betrothed, to Him.

When Joseph then discovered that Mary was expecting, he knew the baby wasn't his. Was there a broken human heart in that painful realization? After all, he was a righteous man who wanted to do what was right before God. How hard it must have been for him to decide to divorce his betrothed. He chose to walk with God into the future, whatever that future held—even if it meant doing it without Mary. But then an angel appeared to him in a dream and conveyed the same incredible news Mary had already received, and we are told that he "did what the angel of the Lord had commanded him and took Mary home as his wife" (Matthew 1:24).

In God's great plan, as they emptied their hands of self and opened their hands to God, He placed their hands into each other's and blessed their obedience in a way far exceeding their expectations. At that point in their journey, He filled them with a growing "measure of all the fullness of God." They were married and together parented Jesus, in whom "all the fullness of the Godhead lives in bodily form" (Colossians 2:9). Talk about being spiritual godparents!

Powerful Transformations

No one will ever replicate the experience that Mary and Joseph shared, yet I believe God has a unique plan for each one of us—one that only you can fulfill. But you won't discover that plan until you take the step of surrender and pray that same prayer: "Lord, what You want for me is what I want for me." It's a prayer that takes us into the godparenting experience and centers us in God's mission and purpose for our lives. Our submission to God enables us to be transformed into a bridge that connects other people with Jesus' abundant life. In fact, this is God's intent for all of us.

Paul wrote: "Those God foreknew he also predestined to be conformed to the image of his Son, that he might be the firstborn among many brothers and sisters" (Romans 8:29). As Christ comes into our lives, He starts transforming us, improving us. Paul later adds: "Do not conform to the pattern of this world, but be transformed by the renewing of your mind" (Romans 12:2). What are we to be transformed into? God's concept is for us to be transformed into transformers—people who use every opportunity to let God's life flow through us to improve the lives of others, fulfilling God's mission.

Florida Power & Light Company has an electrical transformer behind my house. It converts the electrical current from one voltage into another that can provide power for my home and many others in the neighborhood. That's essentially what a spiritual transformer does, too. Spiritual godparents apply the power of God to transform as many hurting people as possible, as soon as possible, by the most effective means possible. When you reach the Godparent stage of maturity, you are so filled with God's life that you want to pass it on to whomever you're with, whatever you're doing, wherever you go.

When you reach the Godparent stage of maturity, you are so filled with God's life that you want to pass it on to whomever you're with, whatever you're doing, wherever you go.

This passion to transform the lives of others was demonstrated by the Apostle Paul. He wasn't limited to just one way of reaching out to others. Everywhere he went, he looked for a way to become a bridge between God and those who did not yet know Him:

> Even though I am a free man with no master, I have become a slave to all people to bring many to Christ. When I was with the Jews, I lived like a Jew to bring the Jews to Christ. When I was with those who follow the Jewish law, I too lived under that law. Even though I am not subject to the law, I did this so I could bring to Christ those who are under the law. When I am with the Gentiles who do not follow the Jewish law, I too live apart from that law so I can bring them to Christ. But I do not ignore the law of God; I obey the law of Christ.
>
> When I am with those who are weak, I share their weakness, for I want to bring the weak to Christ. Yes, I try to find common ground with everyone, doing everything I can to save some. I do everything to spread the Good News and share in its blessings. (1 Corinthians 9:19-23 NLT)

Paul was like a musician who sits in with a band. When someone suggests a song, he says, "What key do you want? I can play it in any key." You'll also notice that Paul is saying, "My life isn't just about me. Now that

I have experienced God's salvation, I need to share it with others." This is the mark of a spiritual godparent.

I read about a woman who was talking with friends over a card game about her recent completion of her First Aid training. They were surprised when she said she had already had an opportunity to use it. She said, "Oh, yes. I was jogging down my street when there was a horrible accident at the intersection right in front of me. I saw the whole thing and heard the screeching tires, a slamming thud, and the crunch of metal." Her friends immediately wanted to know, "What did you do then?"

She replied, "Just like that, my First Aid training kicked in. I sat down on the curb, put my head between my legs, and I didn't even faint!"

Somehow that just doesn't seem right, does it? Most people don't take first aid just to use on themselves. And mature Christians don't just enjoy the benefits of God's great love and the Spirit's gifts without sharing them with others.

What is God's answer to the limitless crash sites of our needy world? You are. You may not see it yet, depending on your stage of spiritual growth, but God sees a purpose for you. He can use you because He sees in you the likeness of His Son, who laid down His life so that others can come to life. He wants to use you to guide and guard others into His marvelous life.

In the recent COVID pandemic, the entire world has been in a season of transition. (By the time you read this, I hope the worst will be over, but the impact of the disease, death, and economic devastation will be with us for many years.) Individuals are going out of their way to stay healthy, yet millions are suffering. Businesses are trying to find ways to avoid bankruptcy. Schools struggle to provide adequate education without unnecessary risk to students. The government is trying to figure out how to help the most people when everyone seems to need help right now. We all realize that we are not where we used to be. But God is still in control, so we can be confident that we're not yet what we are going to be.

The river has moved, so the structures must shift. This is especially true for the church, or it will become a bridge to nowhere, with no connection to the river. What does God want the church to do? I keep hearing the Lord remind me that the church isn't a building, an institution, or a method. The church is His people who are committed to know Him and grow with Him in the river of life, maturing in Him while being filled to the whole measure of His fullness. And after that empowering transformation, we're called to join Him on a mission to a world in need, becoming transformers to help meet those needs.

I've learned a lot about transformation lately from one of my favorite theologians: my grandson, West. At six years old, he's already an expert on the subject. He tells me all about Transformers named Optimus Prime, Bumblebee, Unicron, and others. They're living, human-like robots capable of transforming into animals or vehicles. West has taught me two important lessons. First, something (or someone) that looks quite ordinary often has the potential of transforming into a powerful hero. There's much more to some cars (and people) than meets the eye. Second, you need to watch out for Decepticons. They, too, are Transformers and can be equally hard to spot, but they're up to no good.

Lots of Decepticons lurk in our world today. Even churches harbor too many clones and cookie-cutter "Christians." It seems to get harder and harder for people to know whom they can trust. If we hope to transform people with the power of God that flows through us, we need to be completely trustworthy and true. If someone trusts you and finds you to be true, they'll also be much more likely to trust what you tell them about God. Be a spiritual godparent, a bridge—a transformer. Surprise people by showing them that despite your outer ordinariness, you've been transformed and are now an ambassador for the mightiest force in the universe who provides the power to transform *them*, as well, into the best people they can be.

One Person Makes a Huge Difference

There is only one you. You have something to offer God that no one else has. When you reach the point where you can pray, "Lord, what You want for me is what I want for me," He will show you how to make a great impact for Him. When you do, you're not surrendering your freedom. You're not losing your autonomy. You're not having your individuality swallowed up into a great void out there. Absolutely not! You're discovering the only way to fulfill God's eternal quality of life. You become a value-added feature to others wherever you go. In sharpening your spiritual EDGE, you can help them find theirs. The EDGE that enables spiritual adults to continue to grow is Evangelism, Discipleship, Generosity, and Empowerment. (These are training areas in our church growth track.) As we hone our commitment to those attributes, we're motivated to respond to God and act whenever an opportunity arises.

I believe one of the saddest verses in the whole Bible is Ezekiel 22:30. Jerusalem and Israel had turned their backs on God and the nation was in terrible condition. God was ready to bring judgment, and He told His prophet, Ezekiel, "I looked for someone among them who would build up the wall and stand before me in the gap on behalf of the land so I would not have to destroy it, but I found no one." God was looking for some person of faith among His people who would be willing to become a bridge of life to a world in need. But not a single person in the nation at that time was qualified, mature enough, and able to respond.

Contrast that sad experience to another time in the nation's history and a very different result. A young man named Isaiah heard a similar call from God during another time of great spiritual need. God asked, "Whom shall I send? And who will go for us?" Isaiah had just been agonizing because he felt so unworthy and unclean in God's presence, yet God had taken away his guilt and atoned for his sin. With that change in his life, Isaiah didn't hesitate. He responded, "Here am I. Send me!" (Isaiah 6:8) His response was a shorter version of, "Lord, what You want for me is what I want for me. I want my life to be all about Your life." And it was. From that point forward, Isaiah was a faithful prophet of God.

The situation is desperate in our nation right now. This is not a time when a half-hearted commitment cuts it. We need mature, growing, committed people to respond to the same question God has been asking for centuries now: "Whom shall I send? Who will go for me?" Will He find willing partners who are ready to volunteer? Or will He just hear crickets in the silence?

What will you say to His call?

ADVENTURE PAGES

Pilot's Flight Plan

1. Do you see any comparisons between the Choluteca bridge and the institutional church? If so, what are they?

2. How close do you think you are to being filled to the measure of all the fullness of God? How can you keep growing and moving toward that goal?

3. When was the last time you were a bridge between God and another person? What were the circumstances? How can you make that a more regular experience?

4. Now that you've read about all the stages of spiritual growth, at which stage do you think you are right now? Do you think you have fully moved through all the previous stages and are ready to move to the next stage? Or do you need to keep working on something you haven't yet achieved? Explain.

5. What are three goals you'd like to set for your ongoing spiritual growth? What's the first step you will take toward accomplishing them?

Course Correction

If you only do one thing, do this: Like a project manager, write out your spiritual growth plan for the next five to ten years.

Captain's Log

If you're helping a spiritual godparent grow, I suggest:

➤ Enjoy every minute with that person!

➤ Together, strategize how you can have a greater impact on your church and your community by helping more people grow to the full measure of Christ.

➤ Give this book to the people in your sphere of influence.

EPILOGUE

"I wanna be like him, yes that's my goal,
Like a rock that doesn't roll."

—Larry Norman

Tony Campolo tells the story of a man named Joe, a drunk gloriously converted in a street outreach mission. Before coming to Christ, Joe was known as a derelict who had reached a dead end in his life, but after coming to Christ, everything changed. Joe became the most caring person at the mission. He spent his days there, doing whatever needed to be done. Whatever he was asked to do, he never considered it beneath him. Whether it was cleaning up vomit left by a sick alcoholic or scrubbing filthy toilets, Joe did it all with a heart of gratitude. You could count on Joe to feed any man wandering in off the streets, and if that man was too out of it to take care of himself, Joe would help get him ready and into bed.

One evening, after the mission director delivered his gospel message to the usual crowd of sullen men, heads drooping, one of them looked up, came down to the altar, and kneeled to pray, crying out for God to help him change. The penitent drunk kept shouting, "Oh God, make me like Joe! Make me like Joe! Make me like Joe!"

The director leaned over and said, "Son, wouldn't it be better if you prayed, 'Make me like Jesus'?" The man thought for a moment then asked, "Is He like Joe?"[24]

Becoming more like Jesus is what spiritual growth is all about, but our growth is a process, first in how we view and value ourselves, and then in how we treat others—sharing God's value-added love by meeting needs of people in our world. Many of the mission partnership ministries of our church are evidence of the kind of change I've written about in this book, as Christ Journey people heard God's call and accepted it! ("Your mission from God, should you choose to accept it.") They accepted His mission, said "Yes" to His call, and launched into an adventure with Him.

"Your mission from God, should you choose to accept it."

I'm thinking of Carlos (not his real name), a fighter pilot who defected from his nation's military after refusing to carry out orders that would have resulted in innocent women and children being killed. He came to Miami where he wound up driving a taxi and frequenting strip clubs. One night, angry, lonely, and desperate, he beat his steering wheel with his fists and cried out to God. When he looked up, he saw a sign our church had sponsored with a message that said: "God is on your side." The sign included our number to call for prayer . . . and Carlos called. I watched his life change, and I celebrated the day he joined an organization that flew missionaries into regions so remote they could only be accessed by helicopter. That's a mission from God!

I'm thinking of Pete and Jodi Brennan, who, following God's call, stepped out in faith and cashed in on the sale of their home and savings from a successful career in the grocery business. For over two decades they have served the people in the *favelas* (slums) of Brazil, helping them find hope in Christ and raising up indigenous leaders from their own communities. Their ministry was multi-site before multi-site was a thing in the U.S. They're on mission from God!

David and Chaya Sumanth lost their dear son Paul to a mysterious car accident. He was a pre-med student at the University of Miami, training to pursue a dream to be a medical missionary to the poor. God brought deep healing to their grieving and broken hearts. And now, responding to God's call, for years they have been serving the needs of orphan children and needy families in India and raising up a new generation of young leaders through Paul J. Sumanth Ministries. A mission from God!

Four fifth-grade girls from our church, Abigail Raffalski, Marlee Gray, Eleanor Harley, and Sarah Livingston, were moved to help hungry children in Miami-Dade County. They partnered with us in what is now known as Feed Miami, a community effort to fight food insecurity in our area. In the eleven years of its existence, Feed Miami has gathered 217 tons of food and served 360,000 meals at no charge. "I was hungry and you gave me something to eat" (Matthew 25:35).

I'm thinking of a small business owner and disciple-maker in our church, who, with Clift Brannon and Rudy Hernandez, shared the gospel with General Manuel Noriega in a Miami cell, and Pastor David Wideman (a former school principal and real estate agent) who assisted in Manuel's baptism. When I visited General Noriega in that high security prison, we would always pray together. We would talk about his family. I officiated his daughter's wedding, and he gave her away over the phone. When I told him I got a new motorcycle, his first question was "Harley Davidson?" That's what he rode in his younger years. I was pleased to say "Yes." Jesus said, "I was in prison and you came to visit me" (Matthew 25:36).

Then there's Betty Lara, who after serving as Executive Assistant in my office, sensed God's leading to intervene in the lives of young women abused in sex trafficking. She is now Executive Director of the faith-based Glory House of Miami, through which we have ministered to hundreds of survivors of human trafficking. Through Street Reach, a residential program and a drop-in center, we help in healing and restoration toward new lives of freedom. "I needed clothes, and you clothed me" (Matthew 25:36).

Jim is a volunteer leader in our ministry for those in our church who speak Portuguese. One evening after a worship experience, he came with Jorge, who had a special request. He felt God wanted him to move back to Lebanon and wanted his pastor's blessing. I prayed God would bless and keep Jorge as he said "yes" to this prompting and use Him in fulfilling His will. Then off he went. A few years later, I was invited to be part of a small group of leaders from the U.S. to attend a conference in Beirut for pastors of churches in the Arab nations, following the war in Iraq. On that trip, I met Saeed (not his real name) who had been a Wahabi Sunni in training to be an imam. He told me the story how a man in a store invited him to attend a Christian worship gathering. He protested at first, but he took a New Testament to read so he could learn how his enemies think. To make a long story short, Saeed began the journey to know God's love through Jesus . . . all because a store clerk invited him to go with him to the Christian gathering in Beirut. That clerk's name was Jorge—the same Jorge I prayed for years before. So of course, I told Saeed he was my spiritual grandson! "I was a stranger and you invited me in" (Matthew 25:35). A mission from God!

Imagine your story in this amazing lineup of people who were willing to grow, and then willing to go when given opportunity to respond to "Your mission from God, should you choose to accept it . . ."

I'm thinking of Chris Lane and CityServe, Miami. I'm thinking of Elly Admiral, serving in The Sudan. Of John Churchill, who, following a military career, partnered with us to plant a church and is now Pastor of Missions at Christ Journey. Of Anthony and former Olympian Brittany Gonzalez who work with students at the University of Miami. Of Mark Lesher, who, called into ministry after serving in Vietnam as part of Seal Team One, has now discipled and mentored many others through our years of service together. I'm thinking of younger adults now leading from "generation to generation": Chris Farrington, Mike Patino, Angie Spivak-Lopez, Erik Bennett, and the twins, Geoff and Greg Gackle. I'm thinking of people who have been entrusted with training and opportunity in

Rwanda, Cuba, Haiti, the Dominican Republic, Ecuador, Mozambique, Guatemala, Jamaica, the Bahamas, and more who serve on medical teams, dental teams, construction teams, women's teams, men's teams, teams of teenagers and entire families. I'm leaving out so many names of so many people! Please forgive me if I've overlooked you.

One day, these people and every person who has ever said, "Yes, Lord, I want for me what You want for me" will have the unspeakable joy of hearing their Master say, "Well done, good and faithful servant! You have been faithful with a few things; I will put you in charge of many things. Come and share your master's happiness!" (Matthew 25:23)

What is that "happiness"? Surely, it has something to do with "being filled to the measure of all the fullness of God" in eternity! The thought is breathtaking! Author Frederick Buechner, in an insight I treasure, once observed: "The place where God calls you to is the place where your deep gladness and the world's deep hunger meet."[25] I'm inspired by this, yet all the more, I want to affirm that God's calling on our lives is so much larger than our gladness or this world's needs. As we follow God's call, we are enlarged! As God's image bearers, our capacity to experience and express our Creator and Redeemer grows as we do. He is preparing us for a world to come and the full measure of "all the fullness of God" in eternity!

We began with this vision, hope, and promise, and I'll end with it:

Now to him who is able to do immeasurably more than all we ask or imagine, according to his power that is at work within us, to him be glory in the church and in Christ Jesus throughout all generations, for ever and ever! Amen. (Ephesians 3:20-21)

For more information about the ministries mentioned in the Epilogue, go to:

➤ *Paul J. Sumanth Ministries:* www.pjsm.org

➤ *Feed Miami:* www.christjourney.org/feed-miami

➤ *Glory House of Miami:* www.gloryhouseofmiami.org

➤ *City Serve Miami:* www.christjourney.org/city-serve

➤ *Agape Women's Ministry:* www.theagapenetwork.org

➤ *Pete and Jodi Brennan in Brazil:* amofavelas.pete@gmail.com

➤ *Chaouki Boulos, Lebanon:* www.lfminternational.org

➤ *Chris Farrington, Nicaragua:* losfarringtons@gmail.com

➤ *Elly Admiral in Sudan:* eadmiral24@gmail.com

➤ *Children in Ecuador:* www.amoryesp.org

ENDNOTES

1   Charles Garfield, *Peak Performers* (New York: Avon Books, 1986), p. 294.

2   Graham Kendall, "The iPhone in your pocket has over 100,000 times the processing power of the computer that landed man on the moon," RealClearScience, July 2, 2019.

3   Cited in a blog post, December 1, 2019, D. W. Winnicott once said, "There is no such thing as a baby" . . . "a baby alone doesn't exist." Cited at https://www.istdpnorth.com/blog/tag/Psychoanalysis

4   Found in HELPS Word-studies in Bible Hub App.

5   https://www.youtube.com/watch?v=ZPkey4aX6wU

6   Cited in "Mother Hen Sacrifices Her Life to Protect Chicks," November 17, 2009, https://www.sermoncentral.com/sermon-illustrations/74355/mother-hen-sacrifices-her-life-to-protect-chicks-by-sermoncentral

7   Salary.com, Accessed August 1, 2020, https://www.salary.com/articles/mother-salary/

8   Darcia F. Narvaez, PhD, "The 'On Demand' Life and the Basic Needs of Babies," Psychology Today, March 4, 2018, https://www.psychologytoday.com/us/blog/moral-landscapes/201803/the-demand-life-and-the-basic-needs-babies

9   Gad Saad, PhD, "Do Parents Recognize Their Infants' Cries?" Psychology Today, March 16, 2013 https://www.psychologytoday.com/us/blog/homo-consumericus/201303/do-parents-recognize-their-infants-cries, Accessed August 7, 2020

10   "This Little Light: About the Song," Ballad of America, https://www.ballad-ofamerica.org/this-little-light/ Accessed August, 18, 2020

11   Doug Yeager, "Remembering Odetta, The Voice of the Civil Rights Movement," ascap.com, February 20, 2018 https://www.ascap.com/news-events/articles/2018/02/odetta-legacy

See also https://www.youtube.com/watch?v=7yrB7ePz5CM

12   Pam McAllister, "Ask Her about Hymn(s), February 8, 2018 http://askher-abouthymn.com/what-gospel-song-became-a-civil-rights-rallying-cry/

13   "What Every Child Needs for Good Mental Health," Mental Health America, https://www.mhanational.org/what-every-child-needs-good-mental-health

14   "It Is Good!", Walter Abercrombie, Baylor "B" Association, May 5, 2020, https://blogs.baylor.edu/buletterwinners/2020/05/05/it-is-good-3/

15   "Developing Adolescents: A Reference for Professionals," American Psychological Association, https://www.apa.org/pubs/info/brochures/develop

16   Tika Yupanqui, "Becoming Woman," 1999 http://www.webwinds.com/yupanqui/apachesunrise.htm

17   Sonal G, "17 Coming of Age Ceremonies from Other Cultures," *Babygaga*, May 12, 2016 https://www.babygaga.com/17-coming-of-age-ceremonies-from-other-cultures/

18   Kelly Williams Brown, *Adulting: How to Become a Grown-up in 468 Easy(ish) Steps* (New York: Grand Central Publishing, 2013)

19   Julie Beck, "When Are You Really an Adult?" Atlantic, January 5, 2016 https://www.theatlantic.com/health/archive/2016/01/when-are-you-really-an-adult/422487/

20   "I've Got a River of Life," words and music by L. Casebolt, https://www.hymnal.net/en/hymn/ns/37/1

21   Cited by John C. Maxwell in "Leaving a Legitimate Legacy," July 3, 2013, https://www.johnmaxwell.com/blog/leaving-a-legitimate-legacy/

22   Paul E. Little, *How to Give Away Your Faith* (Downers Grove, IL: InterVarsity Press, 1966, 1988), p. 83

23   "Have Thine Own Way, Lord," Adelaide A. Pollard, 1906, https://hymnary.org/text/have_thine_own_way_lord

24   Tony Campolo, *Everything You've Heard Is Wrong* (Dallas: Word, 1992), p. 73.

25   Frederick Buechner, *Wishful Thinking: A Theological ABC* (New York: HarperOne, 1973), p. 95.

ACKNOWLEDGMENTS

My appreciation and gratitude to the many people who have helped bring this project to fruition.

Special thanks to the creatives on staff at Christ Journey Church who helped shape the framework of this book from its inception as a message series on personal discipleship, including the very "sticky" title Mature-ish. I am indebted to you all for the inspired leadership you bring. Thank you, Charity Betancourt, Jeremiah Pena, Angie Spivak-Lopez, Rosa Aracia, Rafael Bracho, Geoff Gackle, James Martin, Jorge Silvestrini and Melane Spanier. Thank you, Andrea McWhirter, for sharing your insight on Family Ministry age and stage development, and Jeff Reed for your en-thusiastic support of the spiritual growth process included in these pages.

Heartfelt appreciation to those I have been privileged to serve alongside in mentoring others: Pastors Ryan Reed, Rafael Then-Gea, Desi Jimenez, John Churchill, Carlos Fojo, Lance Brown and Jacob Williams. Special thanks to my friends and fellow mentors, recently retired Pastors David Wideman and Mark Lesher. What a joy to serve with you all.

Thank you, Cindy Cohen for the fun family cover art and creative design. And shout out to A.J. and Andy Lopez for the handwriting-on-the-wall inspiration in graffiti art for the series design.

Thank you, Bryan Krause, Vannia Enriquez, Jose Diez, Pat Springle, and Steve Blount for your invaluable assistance in bringing this tool to its printed form. And sincere gratitude to each of the people who, upon review of contents from this book, were willing to offer their kind words of endorsement. Thank you so much!

To the magnificent members of Christ Journey Church who continue to make such impressive strides forward as we follow Jesus together, Thank you for allowing me the privilege of being your pastor. I love you, pray for you, and thank God for the way you support and encourage me, especially for the way you seek to apply the teachings of Jesus so that together we "may be filled to the measure of all the fullness of God."

To Lisa, my wife, who has listened ad nauseum to me as I spouted my way through these ideas as they grew from birth through every age and stage of life. Thank you, Honey, for your seemingly never-ending patience and feedback. You are the best!

ABOUT THE AUTHOR

Bill White is the long time Senior Pastor of Christ Journey Church in Miami, Florida. The multi-thousand member church has multiple physical campuses and Christ Journey Church Online. It's a *glocal* congregation is multi-national and multi-lingual. The church has built schools in the Dominican Republic and Ecuador, homes in Cuba, churches in Rwanda and Haiti, vegetable gardens in the Bahamas, and a medical clinic in India. This past year it assisted in disaster relief after the explosions in Beirut, Lebanon, and the multiple hurricanes that devastated Nicaragua. Locally, it continues its work helping families at risk, single moms, and former victims of drug addiction, domestic violence, and human trafficking. The church is honored to be included in Leadership Network's *400 Gathering* of the most innovative churches in North America. Since its inception in 2009, its *FeedMiami* initiative has gathered and distributed over 217 tons of food, serving over 360,000 meals without charge to the food insecure of Miami-Dade County.

Pastor Bill's community service includes being the past Chairman of the Board of Trustees for Baptist Health South Florida, Vice Chairman of Miami Baptist Hospital, and a board member for the Miami Cancer Institute. He is Board Chairman of Agape Network in its expanding ministry for women and children. An active Rotarian for years, he was honored to receive a lifetime Rotary membership from the downtown Miami Rotary Club. He is also part of the Multi-Faith Neighbors Network, fostering trust and respect among Muslim Imams, Jewish Rabbis, and Evangelical Pastors. He remains active with local leaders in government, law enforcement, and local church and civic leaders in the pursuit of social and racial justice.

Pastor Bill holds three earned degrees: a BA from William Jewell College, and the Master of Divinity and Doctor of Ministry degrees from Southwestern Baptist Theological Seminary. Additionally, he has done post-graduate studies at Baylor University and the University of Virginia.

He and Lisa have two grown daughters and two brilliant grandsons. His adventures include free diving in the Bahamas, waterfall rappelling in North Carolina, mountain biking and hang gliding in the Tetons, skydiving with the Golden Knights, and Harley and horseback riding along the way. Since the writing of his first book, his broken bone count is still ten.

THE BRIDGE TO GOD'S LOVE AND FORGIVENESS

A number of organizations and denominations use a gospel presentation called "the bridge." When you want to tell someone about the life-changing power of Jesus, this method helps you be simple, clear, and accurate. It also follows the thematic flow of the Bible: creation, fall, redemption, and restoration.

1. On the top of the page, draw a line with a person and God on the same line.

Explain: God created us to be in a close, wonderful relationship with Him.

2. Draw a different diagram with a chasm between us and God.

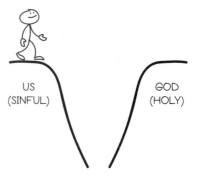

Explain: But there's a problem . . . a big problem. Sin entered the world. Sin isn't just breaking some arbitrary rules; it's choosing to run our own lives apart from God. And we're not alone. The Bible says, "For everyone has sinned; we all fall short of God's glorious standard" (Romans 3:23). Sin has created a huge chasm between us and God, and there's nothing we can do—by being good enough, caring enough, or generous enough—to prove that we're worthy of God's acceptance. That's really bad news, because the penalty for our sin is eternal separation from God. Is there any hope for us? Yes, there is!

3.   Add the cross bridging the chasm.

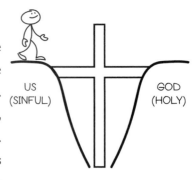

Explain: The good news—in fact, the *wonderful* news—is that Jesus has done for us what we couldn't do for ourselves. He died the death we deserved to die, and He lived the life we couldn't live. "Yet God, in his grace, freely makes us right in his sight. He did this through Christ Jesus when he freed us from the penalty for our sins" (Romans 3:24). Because of what Jesus has done for us, our sins are forgiven and we receive new life in Him. The penalty for sin is replaced by the love of God, and "since we have been made right in God's sight by faith, we have peace with God because of what Jesus Christ our Lord has done for us" (Romans 5:1). Who wouldn't want that?

4.   Add the rest of the words on the diagram.

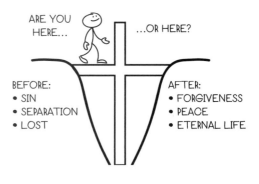

Explain: All of us have a choice—to accept God's gift of grace, forgiveness, and love . . . or not. Jesus promised, "I tell you the truth, those who listen to my message and believe in God who sent me have eternal life. They will never be condemned for their sins, but they have already passed from death into life" (John 5:24). How do we express our belief in God and receive the gift of His grace? One way is by talking with God. Read this prayer, and if it expresses your heart, pray it to God.

Lord Jesus, I need you. I realize my sins have kept me from You, and I need Your forgiveness. Thank you for dying on the cross to pay the penalty for my sins. Thank you for loving me, for forgiving me, and making me Yours.

When we express our faith in what Christ has done for us, some amazing things happen: all our sins—past, present, and future—are forgiven, we're freed from slavery to sin, and God gives us new life, joy, and power. And there's more: we're adopted as God's dear children.

If you've expressed your faith in Christ by accepting His grace, or if you have some questions about what this means, find someone to talk to. You've begun the adventure of walking with the Creator, Savior, and King of the universe. There's nothing better than that!

ANSWERING NON-BELIEVERS' QUESTIONS

It's our privilege and responsibility to help people move along the continuum from unbelief to faith in Christ. If you're new to the field of Christian apologetics and evidences for faith, these are excellent resources to help you start loving God "with all your mind" as well as your heart, strength, and soul.

Apathetic:	*Man's Search for Meaning*, Victor Frankl
Hostile Atheist:	*There Is A God*, Anthony Flew
	The Question of God, Dr. Armand M. Nicoli, Jr.
Rational Atheist:	*Can Science Explain Everything?*, John Lennox
	The Reason for God, Tim Keller
	Making Sense of God, Tim Keller
Ornery Agnostic:	*I Don't Have Enough Faith to Be an Atheist*, Norman Geisler
	Mere Christianity, C. S. Lewis
Honest Agnostic:	*The Case for Christ*, Lee Strobel
	The Case for Faith, Lee Strobel
	The Case for a Creator, Lee Strobel
Open Agnostic:	*Who is This Man?*, John Ortberg
All Seekers:	*More Than a Carpenter*, Josh McDowell
	The Search for the Spiritual, James Emery White
	How Good is Good Enough?, Andy Stanley
	The Bible – You Can Believe It, James C. Denison
	Biographies can also be helpful to reveal how well-known believers came to faith (Tim Tebow, Tony Dungee, Francis Collins, etc.).

RESOURCES

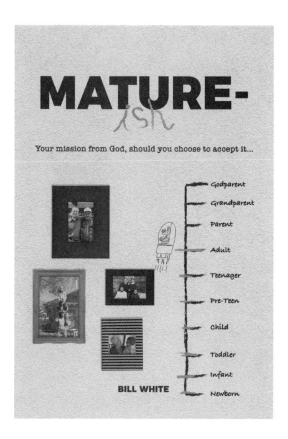

To order additional copies of this book and
to access free video resources visit pastorbillwhite.com

The eBook is available at Amazon.com

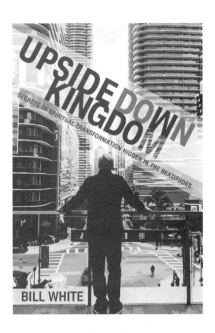

Nine statements . . .

In Jesus' greatest sermon, He begins with the Beatitudes: nine statements that turn our world upside down. He's establishing a counterculture, a different way to seeing reality, with a shocking set of blessings. Jesus is asking us to join Him in a kingdom that challenges everything we normally believe and hold dear . . . and offers us more than we've ever imagined.

Sound intriguing? Hold on tight. Look at this modern translation: "God's kind of happiness comes to those who know they are poor. Divine comfort is showered on those whose hearts are broken with grief. If you are truly meek, the whole world belongs to you. And for those of you who are suffering for doing the right thing—Awesome! It's party time! You belong in God's hall of fame!"

To order copies of this book in either English or Spanish, go to
pastorbillwhite.com

The eBook versions and the audiobook are available on Amazon.com